FOREIGN ARMOUR IN ENGLAND

LECTOR HOUSE PUBLIC DOMAIN WORKS

FOREIGN ARMOUR IN ENGLAND

JOHN STARKIE GARDNER,
VICTOR ALEXANDER FARQUHARSON

ISBN: 978-93-90314-40-9

Published: 1898

LECTOR HOUSE LLP
E-MAIL: lectorpublishing@gmail.com

Plate I.—Painted Wooden Shield of the Fifteenth Century. Burges Collection, British Museum.

FOREIGN ARMOUR IN ENGLAND

BY

J. STARKIE GARDNER

1898

CONTENTS

LIST OF PLATES

LIST OF ILLUSTRATIONS

FOREIGN ARMOUR IN ENGLAND

CHAPTER I

INTRODUCTORY

A former monograph, *Armour in England*, treated of weapons and armour made either in this country or connected historically with English wearers. The more extensive field of foreign armour brought into England by wealthy and enthusiastic collectors is now embraced.

The enthusiasm felt for armour is not surprising; its interest is so many-sided. Not only are collectors fascinated by it, but students of history, artists, and antiquaries. As mere decoration it appeals to some, and finds a place in their abodes; but it is among artistic people that its more ardent admirers are found. Hence it is far from rare to find the glint of arms and weapons lighting up the artist's walls.

From the artistic standpoint nothing can be more picturesque than the varied forms assumed by armour and weapons in obedience to the all-powerful dictates of self-preservation, or to the more arbitrary changes of fashion. To realise what these changes mean, to appropriate them to the scenes and episodes of history, belongs to the painter, sculptor, and scenic artist. If anything in art should be accurately portrayed, it is the men and the events which make up history. Historic painting and sculpture, which might live long in art, may be disregarded by posterity owing to the anachronisms due to neglect of this important study. Most of the changes were perhaps efforts to avert the recurrence of some accident in the lists or field of battle. To definitely track them to their actual origin, to seek out the causes for the singular and ceaseless modifications arms and armour have undergone, is, however, work only possible to the antiquary. It is his province to open the door to the artist.

The quality of the art lavished as decoration on the gala suits of princes and nobles is superb. In mediæval days it was the prerogative of the male sex, the fighting sex, to deck itself like a game bird in gorgeous plumage; women's raiment was more subdued. To the male, no richness of dress that ingenuity could invent or wealth procure was denied. In preparation for those stately festivals when the courtier was to shine in the presence of the fair sex, his sovereign, and his peers, nothing was spared. The armour of parade intended for royal jousts and tournaments is as sumptuous as the wit of man could devise, with time and money unstinted. Chasing, embossing, engraving, damascening, and gilding of the most exquisite quality were lavished upon it, the designs, and possibly the actual work, being by the best artists of the day. The later suits, when cap-à-pie armour was mainly consecrated to festivals and little regarded in battle, were especially loaded with decoration. Besides its excellence of design and richness of ornament, the mere craftsmanship of the armour itself is of a quality that never can be excelled, and the modern counterfeiter, with all his skill and appliances, is baffled in the reproduction of *tours-de-force*, such as the high-combed morions of Italy and Spain.

To study the evolution of armour is like observing the works of nature. Necessity, it is well known, is the great stimulator of the inventive faculty of man, and no necessity is more cogent than that of self-preservation. In the long trials of skill, in which for generation after generation the armourer was pitted against the guilds concerned in the production of lethal weapons, the means of defence seemed once or twice so entirely perfected as to defy the weapons of the assailants. But ere long, the attacking forces, gathering energy, calling on the ingenuity of bowyers, fletchers, sword- and gun-smiths, seem again to emerge triumphant, armed with yet more deadly and powerful weapons. The struggle on the one hand to encase the man, like Achilles, in invulnerable armour, and on the other to break down his armour of proof, was like that between the gunners and naval architects to-day, but it lasted for centuries. It ended, as all such struggles must, in the complete discomfiture of the armourer; the increasing use and accuracy of firearms finally reducing defensive armour to a costly incumbrance. Nature, indeed, seems to will that all things, animate or inanimate, should succumb to persistent attack. Viewed in its true light, armour reveals all the stages, and is the very embodiment of, perhaps, the most prolonged and determined struggle that the development of civilisation has witnessed. It presents a gauge of the extent and limitation of man's inventive faculties, in other words, of his brain capacity, in the ages so-called mediæval.

Concerning the history of the vast bulk of the armour that falls into the possession of the collector, all is speculation, and its very nationality perhaps matter of conjecture. The place whence it has come is often purposely concealed by the dealer, and a legend concocted to invest it with a higher market value. The weapon may have played its part in the stern realities of war; the armour may have saved its owner, or, failing in the hour of need, contributed to the deaths of those who trusted to it. Little armour perished with the wearer. Next to gold and silver, the harvest of arms was the most coveted spoil of victory, and none remained ungleaned on the battle-field. What harvests such holocausts as Flodden Field must have presented, affording opportunities of refitting to the man-at-arms, archer, hobiler, billman, down to the rapacious camp-follower. Though etiquette may have hindered the squire of low degree from donning the full cap-à-pie armour of the knight he overcame, no doubt many a captor of rich armour sacrificed life to indulgence in the dangerous vanity of dressing beyond his station.

The historic and personal associations connected with the arms and weapons present at, and by whose agency were enacted, the decisive battles, the most stirring incidents of history humanity can witness, are not the least of the many-sided interests of armour.

Though but a small proportion of the vast number of suits, helmets, and weapons that have come down to us can be assigned to definite wearers, and most of even these were but the parade suits of royalty and the court, the few pieces of real actual fighting armour identified with particular owners are invested with extraordinary interest. Most of these owe their preservation to the ancient and poetic custom of hanging the arms of knightly personages over their tombs, a custom linked with the still older dedication of arms and armour at the obsequies of the dead, either by placing them in the grave or hanging them in the temples of the gods. The reality of the connection between the pagan and Christian customs is apparent by such incidents as that of William of Toulouse, early in the thirteenth century, who dedicated his helm, shield, and weapons to St. Julian, hanging them over his shrine; or that of the King of France, who, after the battle of Cassel in 1327, presented his victorious arms to the neighbouring church. The churches in fact ought to have been the great treasure-houses for actual armour, as they are of representations of armour on monuments and brasses. Unfortunately, however, the old veneration for the person of the dead which led to the consecration of the armour and weapons he had actually used, hardly survived the close of the thirteenth century. Cupidity induced the prelate to claim them as a perquisite of the burial function, as when the Prior of Westminster received £100 as ransom for the horse and accoutrements of John of Eltham; while the temptation natural to the survivor to retain the finely tempered weapons and armour, whose quality had been tested in the field, had always to be reckoned with. This reluctance to sacrifice them is beautifully expressed in such ancient ballads as those on the death of King Arthur.

Armour was moreover specially devised by will to be kept as heirlooms. Grose in the *Antiquities* states that Thomas Beauchamp, Earl of Warwick in the time of Henry IV., left to his son Richard by will the sword and coat of mail said to belong to the celebrated Guy, Earl of Warwick, he having received them as an heir-loom from his father. Sir Thomas Poynings, in 1369, devised to his heir the helmet and armour which his father devised to him. It also became penal to make away with armour. Enactments, such as that of 1270, commanded that all armour was to be viewed and kept in safe keeping under good security not to be let go, for the king's use at reasonable valuation. The custom, which prevailed extensively, of leaving the undertaker to provide property helmets and arms in place of those the departed had himself used, also tended to lessen the interest of even the arms which yet remain. That the helmet of Henry V. was provided by the undertaker is well known, and that he continued to provide arms down to Elizabeth's time, is shown by accounts of funerals such as of Lord Grey de Wilton in 1562, when among the items of the undertaker's bill are a "cote of arms," banner and bannerolles, a "helmett of stele gylt with fyne golde," with a crest gilt and coloured, a "swerde with the hyltes, pomell, chape, buckle, and pendant, likewise gylte, with a gurdle and sheathe of velvet." This custom of substituting spurious insignia at the solemn interment of the dead was set by the Church, who consigned mock croziers and chalices of no intrinsic value to the graves of even the most exalted prelates. But of the true and the spurious armour alike, time, rust, and above all, changes of religious sentiment in regard to the churches, have spared little besides an occasional helmet. The claims of neighbouring magnates, to the custody of what they regard as family relics, the temptation to sell, and lack of interest, have further sadly reduced this residue within the present century.

Yet neglect and depredations notwithstanding, the preservation of nearly all the English fighting helms known, from the time of the Black Prince to that of Henry VIII., and of many swords of early date, is due to their having been deposited in churches. Other magnificent fourteenth and even thirteenth century swords owe their preservation to their inclusion in the insignia of Municipal Corporations. Lincoln, Bristol, Kingston on Hull, Newcastle-on-Tyne, Southampton, Gloucester, Hereford, Exeter, Chester, Coventry, are among the cities still possessing these interesting relics.

If our national collections are less imposing than those of Spain, Austria, Italy, France, and Germany, the enthusiasm of wealthy amateurs has made this country second to none in the richness of its private collections of European arms and armour.

Of collections commenced and handed down from the time that armour was still in use, by far the most important is the Tower Armoury. Its history can be gathered from Lord Dillon's paper in the fifty-first volume of *Archæologia*, "Arms and Armour at Westminster, the Tower, and Greenwich." The collection had its origin in Henry VIII.'s passion for arms and armour, which was ministered to by Continental sovereigns, especially Maximilian, who shared this taste, and with whom he maintained a close friendship. His extensive array of tilting and jousting suits was kept at Greenwich, and an inventory taken of them upon his death. They were not removed to the Tower until perhaps 1644, though the armoury there was already, during the reign of Henry, one of the sights of London. The arms stored at Westminster were probably removed to the Tower as early as the beginning of the reign of Edward VI. The armoury was no doubt regarded more as an arsenal for use, than in the light of a collection, and perhaps was drawn upon constantly until the Civil Wars, when it was extensively depleted. Five of the Greenwich complete suits of Henry VIII. still exist, however, three mounted upon barded horses, as well as other pieces. The collection becoming on its removal a national one, several suits of distinguished nobles of Elizabeth's reign, and some of the royal armour of the Stuarts, were added. During the present century attempts to render it more complete have been made, by purchasing examples of enriched foreign armour, and more especially of pieces illustrating the armour of more ancient days. Many of the latter, however, are now pronounced to be spurious, and none of them are remarkable.

It appears that the Tower collection has been drawn upon, at some comparatively recent period, for the decoration of Windsor Castle. Some half-dozen of the richest suits are now in the Guard Chamber. Arrayed in cases in the north corridor is a most extensive collection of magnificent weapons, many intimately connected with the history of the country, as well as a matchless collection of oriental arms and armour, formed to a large extent from the collection at Carlton House and added to by Her Majesty.

The Museum of Artillery in the Rotunda at Woolwich contains a valuable collection of armour and weapons, formed partly from the Tower collection, and by judicious purchases. The series of Gothic armour from Rhodes is very remarkable. There are also a few pieces in the Royal Artillery Institution not far distant, and a small part of the collection has been placed in Dover Castle.

The British Museum contains a limited but choice collection, chiefly bequeathed by Mr. Burges, of Mediæval and Renaissance armour, as well as its unrivalled series of antique arms and weapons.

The South Kensington Museum also possesses a few interesting arms and weapons, besides collections deposited on loan.

The munificent bequest of the Wallace Collection has put the nation in possession of a superb series of armour only rivalled by that in the Tower Armoury. It must unfortunately remain inaccessible, being packed away in cases until the rearrangement of Manchester House is completed; consequently none of its contents could be illustrated. It contains perhaps over 1200 specimens, without counting the Oriental arms, all of them choice and some unsurpassed. It is rich in Gothic, fluted, and highly decorated armour, and comprises a matchless series of swords and other weapons. Of private collections in this country that are historic, the Earl of Warwick's is undoubtedly the most interesting, part of it having been in the Castle from the days when armour was in constant use. Besides the few almost legendary pieces, it claims to contain armour of Lord Brooke, killed at Lichfield, of Montrose, the target of the Pretender, and Cromwell's helmet.

Among the armour at Wilton House are the superb suits of the Dukes of Montmorency and Bourbon, captured by the Earl of Pembroke at the battle of St. Quentin, together with the suit worn by the Earl, and pictured in the Jacobe Album. With these are a good number of lancers' demi-suits marked with the family initial. The armour of the Earl of Cumberland, also figured in the Jacobe Album, yet remains in perfect preservation in the possession of Lord Hothfield. The collection at Penshurst Castle comprises some good armour, including helmets and weapons of the Sidneys, its former owners. Sir Wheatman Pearson possesses the barded suit of fluted armour said to have been worn by a Talbot of Shrewsbury at the Field of the Cloth of Gold. Many other ancient seats still contain family armour, either relics of the Civil Wars, as at Littlecote and Farleigh Castle, or removed from the neighbouring church, or discovered in some attic, vault, or even well, as at Arundel.

The Armourers and Braziers Company possess one of the Jacobe suits in their small collection; the Benchers of the Middle Temple own some armour; and there are a few pieces in the United Service Museum in Whitehall. Mr. Leonard Brassey possesses a fine historic cap-à-pie suit of the hereditary challengers, the Dymoke family. Some of the Corporation Museums, especially at Edinburgh, comprise examples of armour and weapons.

It is unfortunate that nearly all the notable private collections made within the present century have been dispersed, either on the death of their owners, or before. The Walpole, Bernal, Meyrick, Londesborough, Shrewsbury, Coutts-Lindsay, Brett, De Cosson, and many other collections have been scattered far and wide under the hammer. The Warwick and others have suffered severely by fire; and of collections made by the past generation probably only that of Lord Zouche at Parham remains intact.

A great deal of armour is absorbed as decoration, not only in such stately homes of the nobility as Arundel, Eaton Hall, Hatfield, Knebworth, but in private houses. Armour is also hidden away in small and unknown collections, like two in the writer's family, which would well repay careful examination. But undoubtedly the richest treasures are in the collections of wealthy amateurs, like Mr. David Currie, Sir Noël Paton, and above all in those of members of the Kernoozer's Club. It is impossible to convey, in a slight sketch, any adequate idea of the wealth of armour in the country, the real extent of which is as yet only to be surmised; but in spite of sales it is doubtless increasing yearly.

The fact cannot be ignored that, of all this mass of armour, very little has been made in England. By far the larger part was indeed certainly made in Germany, a country devoted to metal-working from the earliest periods of its history.

The first dawning of anything like European reputation for the production of arms and armour, since the collapse of the Roman Empire, was achieved by Germany. Owing to its political constitution, and perhaps extent and population, its towns were more enterprising in mediæval ages than ours, and acquired a name for particular manufactures at a relatively early period. The necessity the trading towns were under of arming their citizens to defend their freedom and privileges, amidst the semi-independent princelings and nobles who kept armed retainers and combined to levy blackmail, induced many to take up the manufacture of arms in self-defence, for which they afterwards sought a market among neighbours and abroad. In the thirteenth century, when St. Louis bore a German sword to the Crusades, the names of Cologne, Passau, Heilbronn appear almost simultaneously as seats famous for the production of lethal weapons. Cologne soon assumed the ascendency, at least in English eyes, for its weapons are spoken of with respect in many an early ballad. Thus the battle of Otterbourne is fought "with swords of fyne Collayne," and King Arthur's sword hails from Cologne:—

> For all of Coleyne was the blayde
> And all the hilte of precious stone.

The Duke of Norfolk having sent for armour out of Germany proves that its armour was already regarded as of superior excellence in the time of Richard II. German armour might have been used more largely in England and at an earlier period, but for want of sympathy, perhaps inherited from the Crusades. These, which knitted so many of the races of Europe into close contact, happened not to promote any *camaraderie* between Germany and ourselves. Their Crusades were undertaken independently, or were ill-timed relatively to ours. The unfortunate differences between Richard and the Archduke of Austria, which drained our country of so much gold and silver that even the chalices were melted, rendered Germany unpopular, and the feeling was not improved by the further great loss of treasure on the abortive election of Richard of Cornwall as Emperor. Princely intermarriages were unable to effect a union of hearts, for the Kings of Almayne never come out well in contemporary poetry. Nor was the perpetual presence of enterprising Hansa merchants in factories, such as the London Steleyard, calculated to promote good feeling, though introducing a large bulk of German goods into the country. Steel, itself a German word, was certainly amongst the imports, probably not only as a raw product, but manufactured into articles such as the "Colleyne clowystes" and "Cullen cleavers," and possibly sometimes defensive armour as well. Until late in the fifteenth century, however, the differences between the military equipment of Germany and England is more marked than between that of England and France, which country with the Netherlands formed a natural barrier that only strong common interests would effectively bridge. When bonds of trade began to knit peoples together, German armour, from its excellent quality, divided the market of the world with Italy. The accession of Henry VIII. opened the English market wide to it, his ambition to again dismember France, his alliance with Maximilian and relationship to Charles V. leading to distinct *rapprochements*. Natural inclination and political necessity strongly biassed him in favour of his wife's kinsmen, until his unhappy divorce left him isolated.

Italy vied with Germany in the production of armour, Milan taking the lead. Matthew of Paris heard, in 1237, from a credible Italian that Milan and its dependencies could turn out 6000 men on iron-clad horses. An item in the inventory of Louis Hutin, 1316, is "2 haubergeons de Lombardi"; and that of Humphrey de Bohun, in 1322, mentions Bologna "un haubergeon qu'est apele Bolioun." Italian armourers were established in Paris as early as 1332. Ancient British ballads abound in references to Myllan and Myllen steel. The Earl of Derby, afterwards Henry IV., sent to procure armour from Sir Galeas, Duke of Milan, and when he had selected all he wished for in plated and mail armour, the Lord of Milan ordered four of the best armourers in Milan to accompany the knight to England. In the fifteenth century Milan was able, after the battle of Macado in 1427, to furnish within a few days 4000 suits of armour for cavalry and 2000 for infantry. At a great Spanish tournament held in 1434, only Italian armour and weapons were permitted. Louis XI. and the Duke of Burgundy settled Italian armourers in their dominions. This king seized in 1481 a heavy convoy of cuirasses, sallads, etc., packed in cotton to prevent them rattling and imitating bales of silk, on the way to the Duke of Brittany, giving them to John Doyac as a reward for their discovery. Monstrelet mentions that the Milanese gave corselets and other armour to the Swiss, with the finest promises, before the battle of Marignano. Henry VIII. kept 1000 Myllen swords for the tourney in the Tower, and sent to Milan to purchase 5000 suits of "almain rivets." The most eloquent testimony to the excellence of Milanese arms is, however, to be found in the pages of Brantôme, a very keen observer on all matters military. Milan furnished the finest engraved and most elegant corselets for *hommes de pieds* "tant de M. de Strozzi que de Brissac." "Ce genre de cuirasse legère eut la plus grande vogue à la cour de France"; and "on y approuvoit fort les corselets gravés de Milan et ne trouvoit point que nos armoriers parvinssent à la mesme perfection, non plus qu'aux morions." Strozzi, insisting that his armaments should be Milanese, "pria voire quasy contraignit tous ses capitaines de n'avoir plus autres armes, tant harquebuses, fourniments, que corselets de Milan": while Guise wished his infantry to be armed not with muskets, but good harquebuzes de

Milan—"de bonne trampe pour ne crever." Milanese armourers, like the Gambertis, were enticed to Paris; Pompée a Milanese was selected to teach the King fencing, and Maistre Gaspar de Milan is pronounced "le meilleur forgeur qui jamais eut." Brantôme further describes the troops on their way to relieve Malta, "portant sa belle harquebuze et son beau fourniment de Milan," and adds, "car nous avions passé par Milan, où nous nous estions accommodez d'habillements et d'armes si superbement qu'on ne scavait pour quelz nous prendre, ou pour gentilshommes, soldats, ou pour princes, tant nous foisoit beau veoir."

Plate II.—A Marauder of the "Bandes de Picardie." In the possession of Mr. J. F. Sullivan.

Florence became later a great rival of Milan, and we find Wolsey negotiating with a Florentine for "2000 complete harness of Almayne rivettes at 16s. per set." Brescia was famed for its steel, and probably supplied the vast requirements of Venice, whose arsenals contained, in the seventeenth century, arms for 800,000 combatants. Henry VIII. requested permission from the Doge of Venice, in 1544, to purchase 1500 Brescian harquebuses, and over 1000 suits of horse and foot-armour. Pisa, Lucca, Mantua, Verona, Pistoja also produced armour and weapons of high quality.

Spain, with the most abundant and accessible supplies of the finest iron ores in the world, celebrated for its weapons from the time of the Punic wars, and with the immeasurable advantage of commanding the services of the Moorish steel-workers who were masters of the armourer's craft, ought to have maintained the first rank as armourers of the world. It probably did for centuries supply its own requirements. We find the Spanish warrior under James of Arragon, 1230, sheathed horse and man in mail, with his quilted *perpunto* or pourpoint beneath, and the iron *gonio* or breast-plate above; the iron greaves and shoes, helmet and shield. Thus equipped, the Christian rode down the Moslem by superior weight of man, horse, and arms, the Moors dispensing with pourpoint and breast-plate, and riding unarmoured horses. The helmets were of Zaragossa steel, and James's "very good sword, lucky to those who handled it," was from Monzon and called Tizo, as the more celebrated sword of the Cid was called Tizona. The most dreaded weapon, however, at this time, was the windlass cross-bow, whose bearers were mounted and carried large shields.

Little of the Moorish armourer's work has come down, though they worked steel extensively in Toledo and Seville. No Hispano-moresque swords exist of earlier date than the fifteenth century, and these have richly-worked hilts in the Arab taste. A few Moorish helmets are preserved, also of the fifteenth century, two of which, attributed to Boabdil, are in the Madrid armoury, and are also richly decorated in the Arab manner. The fame of Moorish armour is preserved in the words Morion and Morris pike. The famed swords of Toledo did not obtain renown until the Renaissance, and were not produced after the seventeenth century. Real Spanish armour appears very clumsy, and probably little, if any, was made much after the accession of Charles V. One of the latest suits in the armoury at Madrid is late Gothic in feeling, with a tilting helm of Henry VII., and marked with the poinçon of the city of Valencia.

France is very much in the same position as England in regard to armour, for no city in it ever established any permanent reputation as a seat of manufacture. Louis X. had a Toulouse sword—Louis Hutin's inventory comprises mail from Chambly. Metz, Pignerol, Abbeville are mentioned by Brantôme as producing armour inferior to Italian. Froissart speaks repeatedly of the excellence of Bordeaux weapons, but at the time when Bordeaux was English. The same is true of the Limoges steel. But Paris must after all have been the metropolis of French armourers. The description by Froissart of the battle of Rosebecque, fought in 1382, where the hammering on the helmets of the combatants made a noise that could not have been exceeded if all the armourers of Paris and Brussels had been there working at their trade, shows that these cities were great centres for the production of armour. The names of very few French armourers have escaped oblivion, however; and Italian workmen were employed in France from at least the time of Louis XI. Some beautifully decorated French armour exists, chiefly early seventeenth century, but in France, as in England, most of the armour was probably obtained from Italy and Germany, when once the superiority of their work was definitely established.

Netherlandish armour was always in high repute, and some of the Brussels armourers achieved European fame. It even set the fashion, as we read that Sir Gilbert Talbot, 1353, provided himself with "a curas complete of Flanderis makyng of the new turn for £20." Very few specimens that can be identified as Belgian or Flemish exist, however, in collections.

CHAPTER II

CHAIN MAIL

The immense antiquity of chain mail, and that it originated in the East, are the two facts beyond dispute in its history. Its fine-linked structure exposes, however, the maximum surface of the perishable iron to atmospheric decay, and hence few specimens of great antiquity are known. The two shapeless masses of iron rust in the British Museum, brought from Nineveh by Layard, only reveal on close examination that they were once supple and glittering coats of mail. Whether these are to be assigned to the Nineveh of Sennacherib or to the Sassanian period, they equally claim to be the oldest actual relics of chain mail in existence. The jackets sculptured on the Trajan column are unusually faithful and realistic renderings of chain-mail armour, for the labour and difficulty of an exact reproduction of the minute and complicated repetitions of form into which the links of mail group themselves are generally evaded by a variety of conventional ways of expressing its texture.

The wearers of mail were nomadic horse—Persian, Parthian, and Scythian, and inhabited a belt stretching obliquely from the Caspian in the direction of Scandinavia, the mysterious and imperfectly known amber trade perhaps keeping these peoples in touch. The Viking became acquainted with mail and brought a knowledge of it to Western Europe; his descendants wore it in their expeditions to the East, completing the circle when the mail-clad Crusaders under Cœur de Lion met the mail-clad horse in alliance with the Saracens on the plains of Ascalon. Coats of Eastern mail called gasigans, as told by Geoffrey de Vinsauf, formed part of the spoils of victory taken by Richard, especially on the capture of the great caravan near Galatin in 1192.

Although an immense quantity of mail exists in collections at home and abroad, it can as yet neither be dated nor located upon its intrinsic structure. The links of the Viking suits discovered in the peat morasses of Denmark are as carefully formed as those from Persia or India of the present century. The fashion of the garment is the only guide, but whether the mail is of the period of the garment, or older material made up, cannot be determined. It continued to be used in the West until the seventeenth century, and to a much later time in Eastern Europe; and it is probable that no scrap of such a costly material was ever discarded. It was not passed on and absorbed by foot soldiers, who seem rarely to have cared to use it.

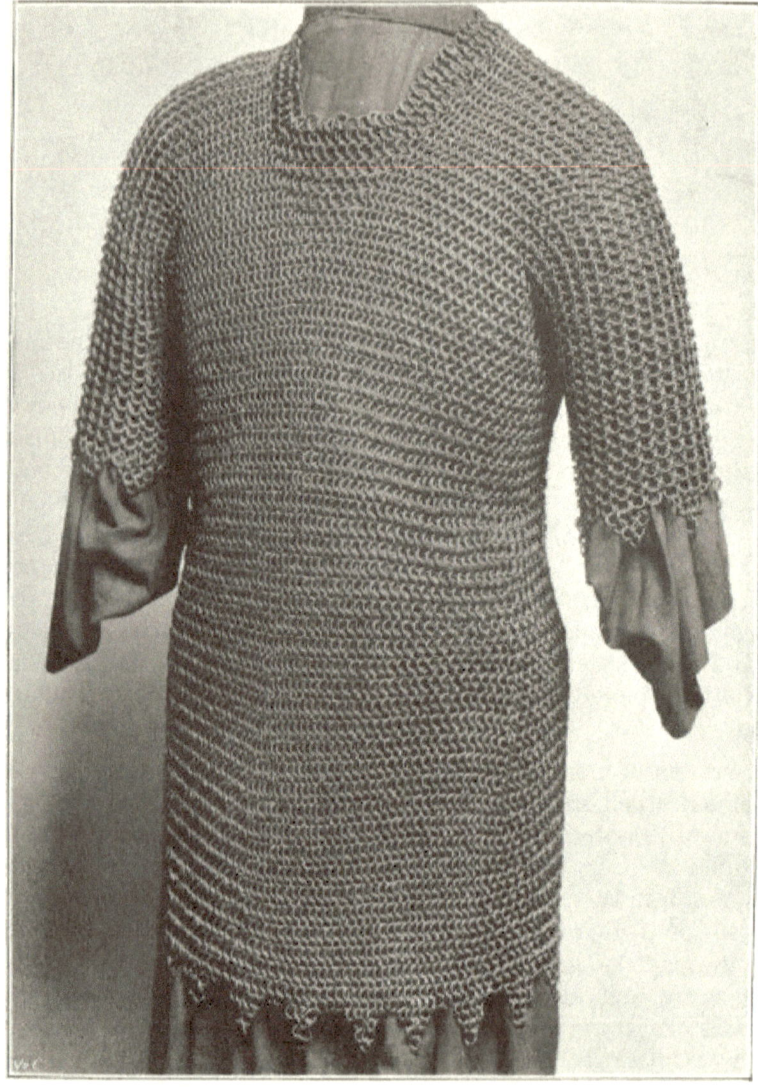

Fig. 1.—Mail hauberk from Sinigaglia. Sir Noël Paton's Collection.

The Norman hauberk did not open down the front, but was drawn over the head by the attendants just before the engagement commenced. Wace relates that Duke William's mail was drawn on wrong side in front in sight of the English. The Norman Duke is the only person represented with leggings of mail in the Bayeux tapestry, and to the absence of these Harold's death and the fate of the day were directly due. His first wound was the turning-point of the battle, twenty Norman knights breaking in and securing the standard. An armed man, says Wace, struck him on the ventaille of the helmet and beat him to the ground, and as he sought to recover himself a knight beat him down again, cutting him on the thick of the thigh to the bone. Girth and Leofwine fell in this onset. The manner of a death which sealed the fate of England must have made a deep impression on the victors, and thenceforth mail chausses became an essential part of the knight's equipment. That any genuine specimens of either the sleeveless or the long-sleeved hauberks of the eleventh or twelfth or even the thirteenth century have been handed down, is improbable. Many mail suits, however, have been acquired in the belief that they were European, and of great antiquity, to the disappointment of their owners, like those adorning the Hall of the Middle Temple, which are modern Persian. One of the oldest, perhaps, is that said to have been found in making a road in Phœnix Park in 1876, and alluded to in *Armour in England*. The oft-repeated statement that it was found associated with a silver badge of the O'Neills has been ascertained by Mr. T. H. Longfield, F.S.A., to be baseless, the badge having been purloined from the ancient harp in Trinity College, Dublin, on which it is now replaced. The hauberk, now in the writer's possession, is of large size and reaches to the middle of the thighs, with short sleeves, and is exquisitely made. Mail shirts, sleeves, etc., of later date than the fourteenth century are far from uncommon, and are represented in every collection. By the kindness of Sir Noël Paton a most perfect fourteenth century specimen is illustrated. It is close fitting, and was exhibited in 1880, and described by Burgess as "one of the few coats of mail which have any decided history." In Meyrick's *Critical Enquiry* we are told that "it had been purchased by a Jew from an ancient family at Sinigaglia, near Bologna, in whose possession it had been beyond any of their records." A note further informs us that "the Jew bought it by the ounce and paid for it forty guineas." Sir Samuel Meyrick observes that it corresponds to the coat of mail on the statue of Bernabo Visconti at Milan. It may be described as a single coat of mail with no slits and no reinforcement. It measures 2 feet 9 inches from the top of the collar, and has sleeves which are 10 inches long from the armpit. "It is wider at the bottom than at the waist, two gussets being inserted for this purpose. The rings average a good half-inch in their interior diameter; half are riveted and half are continuous, the latter have a pear-like section, the rounded parts being on the inside circumference. The riveted rings appear to have been made of circular wire, but have become rather flattened, probably by wear. The rivets are of the pyramid shape, like those of the Dublin coat of mail, but much bolder and larger. There is a row of brass rings round the neck, and the bottom of the edge and sleeves are finished by vandykes, also in brass rings, riveted with iron. This is probably the finest coat of mail that has come down to us." One of the figures guarding the Maximilian cenotaph wears a precisely similar hauberk. Italian pictures in the National Gallery show that the custom of finishing off mail defences with several rows of brass links, to form some sort of scolloped edging, was universal in Italy during the fifteenth and sixteenth centuries. French and English monuments and manuscripts prove that this custom extended to Western Europe, the scolloped edge commonly showing over the tassets from beneath the pourpoint.

Vestiges of the camail are found on fourteenth century bassinets just as they are seen in the conical helmets from Nineveh and on the Trajan column. The standing collar or gorget superseded it. Fig. 2 reproduces a perfect specimen belonging to the Royal Artillery Institution at Woolwich, of exquisite work, with the links round the throat reinforced or doubled. Though gorgets of plate were introduced as early as 1330, many still preferred to wear the mail, so that they continued more or less in use for two centuries longer. Mail was generally worn bright. In the fourteenth century *Anturs of Arthur* we read:

> His mayles were mylke quyte, enclawet full clene
> His stede trappet with that ilke, as true men me told.

An early fourteenth century stanza, the 39th of the "Armynge of King Arthur," suggests that the surcoat over mail was to keep off rain and not sun. The colour green was almost universally used from the reign of King John.

> With scharfe weppun and schene
> Gay gownes of grene
> To hold theyr armour clene
> And werre it from the wette.

For a brief period in the sixteenth century, mail was again worn without plate armour. The custom was revived in Italy when assassination was rife, and is seen in portraits of Italian noblemen in the National Gallery.

Fig. 2.—Standard Collar of Mail. Royal Artillery Institution.

The costume of the unfortunate Wyatt on his rebellion is described in the chronicles of Jane and Queen Mary as "a shert of mayll with sleves, very fayre and thereon a velvet cassoke and an yellowe lace with the windelesse of his dag hanging thereon, and a paire of botes and spurres on his legges; on his hedd he had a faire hat of velvet with broade bonne-work lace about it." Soon after a "shippe laden with shertes of mayll" was brought in by Strangwyshe the Rover, "who came from the French king and submitted to the Queen's mercy." The celebrated duel between Jarnac and La Chateigneraye was fought in shirts of mail.

In the Scottish wars of Edward I. it was a common saying that "arrows can penetrate the hardest mail"; and more efficient armour had to be devised. Simon de Montfort, standing like a tower and wielding his sword with both hands, was pierced in the back by a foot soldier who lifted up his mail. The hero died with "Dieu merci" on his lips; not the only victim who met his death in this manner. The change in the fashion of armour was hastened by such events. The process has already been traced: it began at the knee-caps, which were covered by plates called poleyns. Three actual and perfectly unique specimens of these, belonging to Sir Noël Paton, show that they were not laid upon or over the mail, but replaced it, as represented in monumental effigies. One pair with parallel sides is finely embossed and vandyked, closely resembling those of some early fourteenth century effigies. A globose example formed of three articulated plates is still more interesting, having been richly damascened with an arabesque design worked in thin brass lines, the field being delicately and closely cross-hatched with incised lines. The really remarkable and unexpected surface decoration this discloses explains the nature, and confirms the accuracy, of certain fourteenth century representations of black armour covered with fine gold arabesques. The cross-hatching served to retain the black pigment, and gave a dark cast to the steel surface, enhancing the value of the delicate brass inlay.

The process of reinforcing the mail defence was continued, as we have seen, until it was entirely cased with an outer shell of plate. A quilted coat was worn beneath the mail, if not a second one between the mail and plate armour. These multiplied defences must have made active fighting difficult and most fatiguing, and were discarded so soon as a light armour of fine steely quality, and without crevices, was procurable.

CHAPTER III
GOTHIC ARMOUR

Plate armour reached the perfection of workmanship in the second half of the fifteenth century. At no period was it so light, yet impervious, with curves and angles so admirably directed to deflect the impact of sword or lance, and articulations so skilfully devised to mitigate the restraint on freedom of movement necessarily imposed by a sheathing of steel. Never was armour so closely fitted to the contour of the body, and thus so elegant, so easily and therefore so constantly worn. This, the so-called "Gothic Armour," is the cynosure of collectors, and is so rarely to be obtained that a fairly perfect cap-à-pie suit may command some £2000.

This Gothic armour is the armour of the Van Eycks and Memling, of Perugino and Leonardo, and of the earlier works of Albert Dürer. The sumptuously illuminated French and English manuscripts of the fifteenth century depict it in use in every vicissitude of war or combat, by sea and land, on horse and foot, and testify how little it impeded the freedom of action of the wearer. They show that it was rarely concealed in campaigning by any textile garment, and also that when worn by prince or noble, it might be gilded, entirely or partially, even almost fantastically. Thus the upper half may be gilt, and the nether limbs left burnished steel; or these gilt and the body steel; but more often the alternate plates of the articulated breast and back defences, the arms, or the elbow and knee pieces, are gilt, while the rest presents the normal sheeny surface of steel.

The general characteristics of Gothic armour have been described in *Armour in England*, illustrated in Fig. 19, by the fine and accurately modelled suit of the Beauchamp effigy at Warwick. Though many fine suits have been brought to this country from abroad, none are in any way connected with English wearers, and none could therefore be illustrated in the former monograph. It seems incredible that nothing should have been preserved either of the weapons or armour with which the long struggle for supremacy in France was maintained during the minority and rule of a king, too studious and placable for days when his turbulent subjects cared only for war. Of the armour and weapons of the thousands of men-at-arms who fell victims to the Wars of the Roses, the direct outcome of the disappointing issue of the French Wars, and so annihilating to English art, perhaps but a helmet and a few weapons remain. The extermination of the old nobility; the completeness of the change in habit and thought introduced into this country by the Renaissance, affecting alike art, literature, and costume; the change in religion, the revolution in the science of warfare, and the absolute centralisation of the ambitious and luxurious nobility in the court or camp of Henry VIII., together with that vainglorious and wealthy despot's passion for extravagant dress, novelty and pomp, combined to break most effectually with the past and to render all Gothic armour mere obsolete lumber. Contemporary pictures of Henry VIII.'s proceedings, especially of his meeting with Maximilian, in which the English retinue is equipped in the new closed armet while Germans wear the old visored sallad, as well as the accounts of his forces and his purchases of arms, convince us that out-of-date armour and weapons, even if still serviceable, were no longer, as heretofore, passed on to the lower ranks of retainers. Hall relates of the muster of the city bands in the thirty-first year of Henry VIII. that "all were put aside who had Jackes, coates of plate, coates of mail, and bryganders, and appointed none but such as had whyte harness, except such as should bear the morish pykes, which had no harness but skulles." The destruction of obsolete armour in this reign must have been very complete, for no suits of the Gothic armour worn down to this date by the fathers and grandfathers of the courtiers of Henry have been preserved.

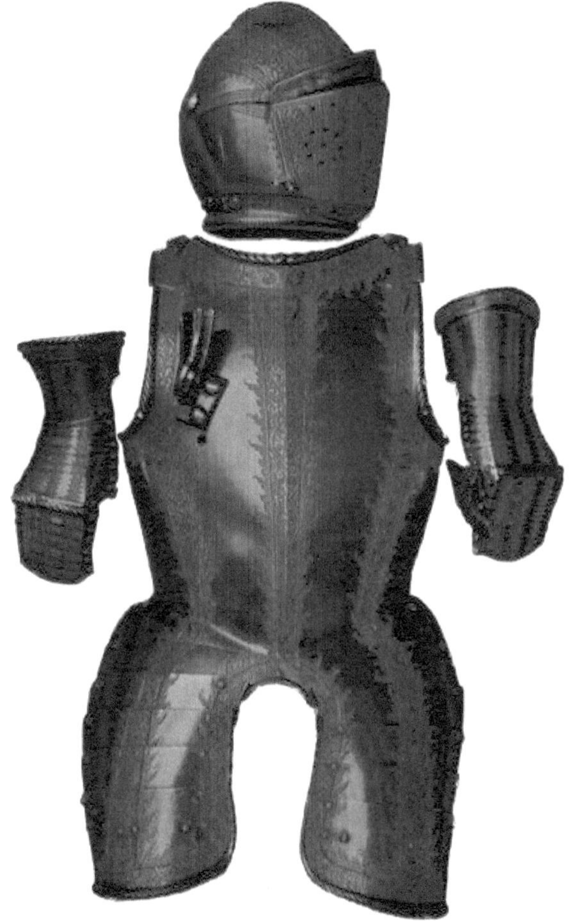

Plate III.—Half Suit, engraved and parcel-gilt. Collection of the Duke of Westminster.

France and the Low Countries have been swept nearly as bare, anything that might have been spared by former ages having been finally destroyed when the houses of the nobility were gutted during the Revolution. In more conservative Italy and Spain a few Gothic suits have escaped destruction, and though the Art Renaissance of the one, and wealth and pride of the other, were inimical to the preservation of obsolete arms, yet probably some few specimens have passed from the hands of private possessors into those of wealthy amateurs of France and England. Germany, however, has ever been the inexhaustible treasure-house whence Gothic arms and armour have leaked from the hands of private possessors into those of collectors. In Germany even the trading towns had clung to their ancient buildings, walls, and traditions, and in many of the old Town Halls the furniture, arms, and weapons of the civic guards, and the old implements of punishment and torture, are still preserved. The innumerable feudal castles of the lesser nobility have to a yet greater extent preserved the belongings of their ancient occupants, who clung to their titles, heraldry, arms, and weapons as symbols of vanishing rights and power, and of ancient pretensions and privileges, so out of harmony with the world beyond. The ubiquitous and assiduous dealer has long found in them a happy hunting-ground for arms and weapons, whence to obtain the bulk of those he disposed of.

In addition, some important stores of Gothic armour have been disgorged from the Levant, trophies of the incessant wars maintained by the Turks against Christendom. A large quantity existed at Constantinople, and the story goes that a ship, some fifty years ago, was actually freighted to Genoa with old armour as ballast. The indefatigable dealer Pratt of New Bond Street became possessed of some of this armour, which he made up into suits in the best way he could, restoring but too liberally the parts that were missing. The suit illustrated, Fig. 3, is in Lord Zouche's collection at Parham, where it is catalogued as from the Church of Irene at Constantinople: it no doubt formed part of this consignment. The head-piece, an Italian sallad, is of later date, while the remainder, though so beautiful in form, does not appear to be either entirely homogeneous or complete. Other suits in Lord Zouche's extensive collection are from the same source. Another much smaller series of Gothic armour was brought to England from the Isle of Rhodes and most fortunately did not pass through the hands of any dealer, and is thus in an absolutely trustworthy condition, the very rust not having been removed. It consists of a number of pieces, approximately of one date, many of particular elegance and interest, both on account of the armourer's marks, and the examples of engraving they present.

By the kindness of Sir Noel Paton two of his four fine Gothic cap-à-pie suits are illustrated. The first, Figs. 4 and 5, is German work of the second half of the fourteenth century.

Fig. 3.—Gothic Armour, said to be from the Church of Irene at Constantinople. At Parham.

Sir Noël observes that "the upper part of the suit especially is remarkable for its perfect condition, the original straps being intact, and the inner and outer surface of the metal having been scarcely touched by rust." The graceful and doubly articulated and engrailed breast and back-plates are beautifully designed, and finished in the manner of the great master armourer Lorenz Colman of Augsburg. The curiously plain collar is attached to the pectoral by a bolt and staple, and there is a fixed lance-rest, these appliances adapting the suit for tilting rather than war. There are no tuilles, one of the most persistent features of Gothic suits, and no pauldrons or shoulder-guards. The brassards, coudières, genouillières, formed of an unusual number of plates, and especially the gauntlets, are of great beauty, and resemble those of Lorenz Colman's suits. These and the *solerets à la poulaine retroussé*, to quote Sir Noël's description, "are exceptionally beautiful and artistic in design. Of the sollerets, however, unfortunately only the left, with its fine, long-necked spur silvered and thickly patinated, is genuine." "The head-piece is a strong bassinet of the type styled barbute by Viollet le Duc, and possibly of somewhat earlier date, and bears on either side the armourer's mark." The fine preservation of the metal "is due no doubt to the fact that the suit had remained for many generations in one place—an old mansion in the northern Tyrol, whence so late as 1872 or 1873 it was obtained by a well-known Parisian dealer, from whom it passed to Pratt of New Bond Street; after whose death it came into my hands."

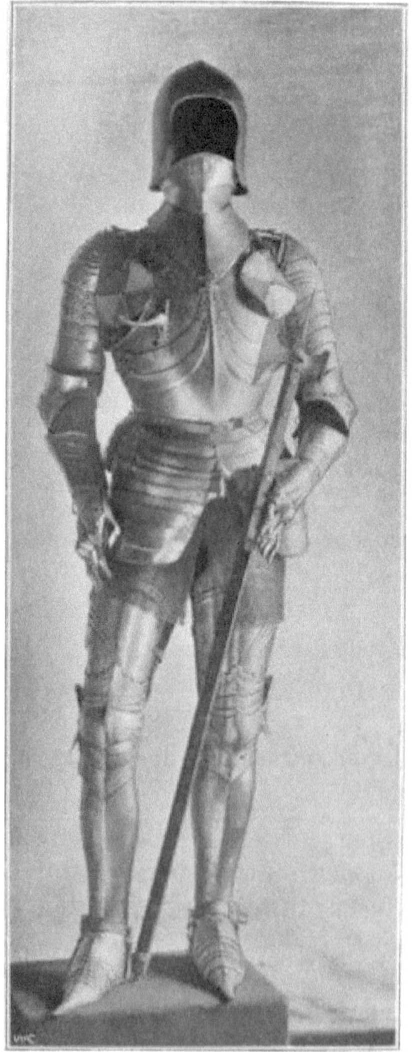

Figs. 4 and 5.—Gothic Armour. Said to be from an old mansion in the Tyrol. Front and Back views. Sir Noël Paton's Collection.

The second of Sir Noël's suits (Fig. 6), of about the same date, resembles more the armour of Italian pictures and actual Italian suits. The articulated and channelled breast-plate is remarkably bold and graceful in its lines, as are the entire brassards, more especially the coudières. "The spiked rondelles and the gauntlets have much picturesque character, and the tuilles are exceptionally fine in form. The sollerets are of the kind called *arc tiers point*. The head-piece is a close helmet of good design and apparently contemporary." In general effect the armour is light but dignified: though the breast-plate bears a Gothic R, no history attaches to it.

The great interest and beauty of the Parham suit, Fig. 3, lies in the particularly elegant and finely laminated and engrailed breast and back-plates. Like Sir Noël's German suit, it has no tuilles and retains the staple for fastening the collar and the lance-rest. The sollerets and perhaps some other pieces are restorations. It is without armourer's marks, but resembles Nuremberg work in general form and detail.

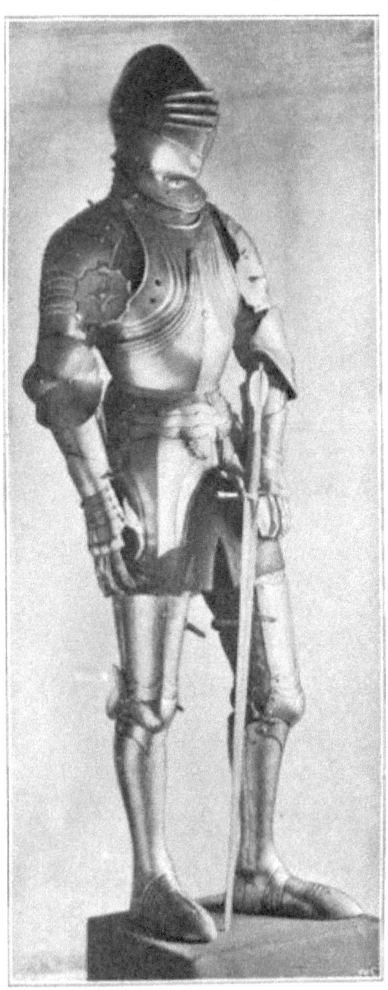

Fig. 6.—Gothic Armour. Probably Italian. Sir Noël Paton's Collection.

Two magnificent Nuremberg Gothic cap-à-pie suits are in the Wallace Collection, at present inaccessible. One is on foot, partly fluted, consisting of sallad with movable visor, mentonnière, jointed breast and back-plate, and quite complete body armour with pointed-toed sollerettes, and skirt of riveted mail. The other, for man and horse, is equally complete and ornamented with brass bands, the sallad with visor and mentonnière being of fine form and contemporary.

Plate IV.—Gold damascening on russet ground. Late Italian suit. Tower of London.

Fig. 7.—St. Michael. By Perugino. National Gallery.

For suits of Gothic armour which have belonged to known wearers, and have been handed down with unbroken pedigree, we must go to the great collections of

Europe, and especially to those which, like the Viennese, were commenced while armour was still worn. Of sculptured representations of Gothic armour none surpass the Beauchamp effigy at Warwick. A no less accurate figure is that by Peter Vischer, also in gilt bronze, of Count Otto IV. of Henneburg, 1490, from the Church of Romhild in Thuringia. There is a cast of this in the South Kensington Museum, as well as one of the gilt bronze effigy of Count Weinsberg at Munich, in armour which is remarkable in several respects. Italian Gothic armour of different periods can best be studied in the National Gallery. A suit (Fig. 7) of about the close of the century is from one of the compartments of the famous altar-piece by Perugino, removed from the Certosa at Pavia in 1786, and painted according to Vasari about 1490. It represents St. Michael in full armour, except the head. The underlying mail shows, as usual in Italian pictures, at the elbows, the skirt, and below the knees, and has a deep edging of brass rings. The breast-plate, though in two, is arranged so that the body could not easily be bent. The shoulder-guards are less exaggerated than in contemporary French and English armour, but the elbow-guards seem large, angular, and loosely fitting. The sollerets are well made, unpointed, and leave the red stocking exposed at the toe and heel. The sword, on the left hip, is in a velvet scabbard with a beautifully and simply worked steel hilt and cross quillons slightly curved towards the blade. The shield is fine in form and typically Italian, bearing a Medusa's head and other classic ornaments, boldly embossed. The hands are bare, the right holding a slender staff or wand. In the figure of St. William by Ercole di Giulio Cesare Grandi of Ferrara, the head is bare and there are no plate defences to the neck, shoulders, or forearms. The top of the mail shirt shows as a narrow band round the throat, and covers the shoulders with short and very wide-open sleeves, its lower edge appearing between the tuilles over a second skirt of mail. Mail appears again below the knees and forms the covering of the feet, all edges being finished with rings of brass as usual. The breast-plate is large, plain, and of one piece; there are but three taces, with bold, finely formed, and ridged tuilles. The brassards, including the large butterfly-shaped coudière, appear from beneath the widely open sleeves of mail. The leg armour is also plain, but with the wings of the genouillières exceptionally large. The sword, unsheathed, is a magnificent weapon with gilt or brass pommel and grip and horizontally curved quillons. The striking figure of St. George by Pisano, in the broad-brimmed Tuscan hat, is of earlier date, as the artist died in 1451 or 1452. The mail shows beneath a thick quilted surcoat over which the great ill-fitting shoulder and other body defences are fixed. The limbs are almost completely sheathed in plate over the mail, but the pieces fit so loosely that the whole has a shambling appearance and seems ready to fall off. The sollerets are square-toed with long rowelled spurs. The armour represented in Boccacino's Procession to Calvary is almost identical, save that the mail sleeves are less baggy and shoulder pieces are worn. The St. William in Garofalo's Madonna and Child from Ferrara, though probably painted in the 16th century, preserves the exaggerated butterfly wings to the coudières and genouillières, and the Gothic tuilles, but has fluted sollerets and shows no mail. The St. Demetrius of L'Ortolano, who painted in the first quarter of the sixteenth century, shows fluted shoulder pieces and coudières, and half sollerets, leaving the front of the foot to a defence of mail.

Fig. 8.—The Battle of Sant' Egidio. By Uccello. National Gallery.

The most interesting picture in the National Gallery (Fig. 8) to the student of armour, however, is that representing the battle of Sant' Egidio by Uccello, fought in 1416, when Carlo Malatesta, Lord of Rimini, and his nephew Galeazzo, were taken prisoners by Braccio di Montone. Uccello was born in 1397 and died in 1475, but there is no evidence as to the year in which the picture was painted. It appears to represent an attempt to rescue the Lord of Rimini, by a knight clothed cap-à-pie in very advanced plate armour and wielding a horseman's hammer. The breast and back plates are articulated; tuilles, where worn, are very short; the large pauldrons are of very varied construction, and either roundels or coudières with butterfly expansions are worn indifferently; in all cases the figures are completely cased in plate armour, though some wear mail gorgets, except that Malatesta has been partly disarmed and is protected by mail alone. De Commines observes that it was the law of arms in Italy to strip those taken to their shirts and dismiss them. The chief interest lies in the head-pieces, which, except in the cases of the prisoners and some trumpeters, are closed armets with baviers and visors hinged at the side, of varied form, the occularia being in all cases notched out at the upper margin of the visor and forming either round or half-round holes or slits. These armets are provided with most fantastic crests and plumes, the crown of the helmet being in several cases covered with velvet, overlaid with goldsmith's work and merging into the crest. All have the roundels at the back of the neck.

Fig. 9.—Carved Relief for the Visconti Tomb in the Certosa at Pavia. South Kensington Museum.

Another notable representation of an Italian battle (Fig. 9), in which the mounted combatants are clothed in complete typical Gothic armour, is to be seen in the cast from the Visconti Tomb of the Certosa, Pavia, in the South Kensington Museum. The armour is of the most beautiful type, and the figures are singularly supple and full of action. The armet is more fully developed and almost uniform in type. The visor works on pivots, the occularium is a slit above it, and the bavier is a separate piece fastened by straps at the back. The event represented is the battle before Brescia in 1402. As a full-sized representation of the latest Italian Gothic armour nothing can perhaps be finer than the fifteenth century effigy of Guidarello Guidarelli surnamed Braccioforte from Ravenna, of which there is also a cast in the South Kensington Museum. The tuilles are flexible and pointed, formed of narrow horizontal plates; the shoulder-plates are bossed into lions' heads; and the armet has a double visor without bavier.

The statue of St. George, made by Donatello for the Florentine corporation of armourers in 1416, is almost Roman in costume and of little interest.

The account of the almost contemporary battle of Fornovo, 1495, by Philip de Commines bears testimony to the excellence of this Italian armour, especially of the close armets. The flower of the allied forces of Italy consisted of 2500 men-at-arms under the Marquis of Mantua, Count di Cajazzo, and Signor John Bentivoglio of Bologna, with other nobles, all well barded, with fine plumes of feathers and bourdonasses, or hollow lances, brightly painted, and used in tournaments. Great bodies of men-at-arms were in reserve. The French van contained 350 men-at-arms, 200 mounted crossbow-men of the king's guard—who fought on foot, however—300 archers and 3000 Swiss foot, several of the highest nobility dismounting to fight amongst them. In the main body were the king's guards, pensioners, 100 Scottish archers, about 900 men-at-arms, and 2500 Swiss, the whole army not exceeding 9000 men. The Italian men-at-arms delivered a charge, with lances couched, at a gentle gallop; the Estradiots, who should have supported them with their scimitars, retired to plunder the sumpter-horses; whereupon the men-at-arms who had charged and broken their lances fled, and their infantry gave ground. Those who had not charged also threw away their lances and fled, sword in hand, and were pursued and cut up. With the French were "a great number of grooms and servants, who flocked about the Italian men-at-arms, when they were dismounted, and knocked most of them on the head. The greatest part of them had their hatchets (which they cut their wood with) in their hands, and with them they broke up their head-pieces, and then knocked out their brains, otherwise they could not easily have killed them, they were so very well armed; and to be sure there were three or four of our men to attack one man-at-arms. The long swords also which our archers and servants wore did very good execution." The losses on the French side were but three gentlemen, nine Scottish archers, twenty horse of the vanguard, and some servants. The Italians lost 3500 men on the field, of whom 350 were men-at-arms, including six or eight of the Marquis of Mantua's relatives and other persons of quality. The lances "lay very thick upon the field, and especially the bourdonasses; but they were good for nothing, for they were hollow and light, and weighed no more than a javelin, yet they were finely painted."

Battles in England were much more serious affairs and were stubbornly contested. Those of the Wars of the Roses opened with a cannonade, after which the archers engaged and the billmen followed, nobles fighting on foot in their ranks to encourage them. Lord Richard Herbert "twice by fine force passed through the battaill of his adversaries," at Banbury, "polle axe in hand": at the battle of Towcester many were taken because they left their horses and decided to fight on foot. The Earl of Warwick dismounted at Barnet to "try the extremity of hand strokes"; but penetrating too far among the enemy to encourage his men, and not being properly supported, he was slain.

At Bosworth the archers formed the forward on both sides. Richard's archers "with a sodein clamour lette arrowes flee at theim. On the other syde they paied theim home manfully again with the same. But when they came nere together, they laied on valeauntly with swordes." The Earl of Oxford, however, kept his men in close order, and the enemy gave way, wholesale desertion sealing the fate of the battle. Henry was not engaged, but kept afar off "with a fewe companye of armed menne." Richard on horseback made a desperate attempt to get at him, but was unsupported and slain.

The English costume is described in the Plumpton Correspondence, when the Archbishop of York, having dues to collect in 1441, quartered 200 men-at-arms in Ripon and held it "like a towne of warre." These borderers wore "breast-plate, vambrace, rerebrace, greves and guischers, gorgett and salett, long spears and lancegayes." English levies were not always so well armed. The 5000 men who came down from the north in the reign of Richard III. were "evell apparelled and worsse harneysed in rustic harneys." Under Henry VII. the Duke of Bedford took out "3000 mene which were harneysed but barely, for theyr breste plates were for the most parte lether." The array taken to Calais by Edward IV. in 1475 is in striking contrast to this. Hall relates that "the men were so well armed and so surely in all things appoynted and provided that the Frenche nació were not onely amased to behold them, but much more praysed them and there order. In this army were 1500 men of armes well horsed, of the which the moste parte were barded and rychely trapped, after the most galiard fashion, havyng many horses decked in one suyte. There were farther 15,000 archers beryng bowes and arrowes, of the which a greate parte were on horsebacke. There were also a great number of fighting men and others, as well to set up Tentes and Pavillions, as to serve their Artilarie." De Commines adds that the men-at-arms, comprising the flower of the English nobility, were richly accoutred after the French fashion, well mounted, most of them barded, and each one with several persons in his retinue.

This Gothic armour, the lightest and most graceful ever produced, was ideal so long as it was customary for men-at-arms to fight indifferently on foot or mounted. The mixed tourney was still in vogue, fought the first day with sharp spears, the second day with swords, the third on foot with poll-axes. The Lord Scales and the Bastard of Burgundy, and the Duke of Albany and Duke of Orleans fought such tourneys, the latter having the misfortune to kill his antagonist by a spear-thrust. It was, in battle too, most honourable to fight on foot among the archers, and there was always a large number of gentlemen volunteering among them to "encourage the infantry" and make them fight the better. "The Burgundians had learnt this custom from the English when Duke Philip made war upon France during his youth for two-and-thirty years together without any truce." De Commines adds that at Montlhéry the order was given to the Burgundians that every man should alight without any exception. Knights equipped by the most renowned of the armourers of Italy and Germany were almost invulnerable until overthrown; but English and Burgundian armour was not an equal protection, as the rash Duke of Burgundy, who seems to have had all his armour home-made at Dijon or Hesdin, discovered to his cost on the field of Nancy, when his skull was cloven by a halberd, and two pike-thrusts penetrated the lower part of his body.

Plate V.—Breastplate, embossed and parcel-gilt. French. Collection of Mr. David Currie.

This fashion of armour appears to have been devised in the ateliers of the Missaglias of Milan. A work by Wendelin Böheim, custodian of the Imperial collections of armour in Vienna, published last year in Berlin (*Meister der Waffenschmiedekunst vom xiv bis im xviii Jahrhundert*), gives a short biographical sketch of this renowned family of armourers, who migrated to Milan towards the middle of the fourteenth century, from Ello, a village not distant from Asti and Lake Lecco. Petrajolo da Missaglia, the founder of the family, settled in Milan as an armourer towards the middle of the fourteenth century, and built the house in the Via degli Spadari where his sculptured poinçon or armourer's mark is still to be seen. The work of his son Tomaso da Missaglia greatly augmented the already world-wide reputation of the armour of Milan, and deserved in 1435 the recognition of Filipo Maria Visconti, who freed him in 1450 from taxes until his death somewhere about 1469. The armour by him is plain, the best known being that at Vienna of the Palsgrave Frederick the Victorious about 1450, with closed helm, roundels, unfingered gauntlets, and pointed sollerets over 13 inches in length. The suit is less graceful than German Gothic armour. The equally renowned son of Tomaso, Antonio, was born about 1430, assisting in his father's extensive business at the age of twenty. Large commissions were received, such as that in 1466, of the value of 20,000 lire, for 100 harness for the ducal mercenaries, and others from Duke Francesco, the Pope, Don Alfonso of Arragon, afterwards King of Naples, etc. On his father's death in 1469, their great patron the Duke presented him with an estate and mill, and in 1470 he added the iron mines near Canzo to his patrimony. Soon after, in 1492, a Venetian envoy sent home an account of Missaglia's works, finding finished harness to the value of many thousand ducats. His death took place near the end of the century; the exact date being unknown, like the name of his immediate successor. There are mentions of several Missaglias about whom little is known, one working in 1466 for Louis XI. Antonio was the last to bear the name of Missaglia, succeeding members of the family assuming that of Negroli, a name first met with about 1515, when a Giovanni Negroli appears as master of the works. The tomb in St. Satyro, Milan, preserves the inscription *Negroli da Ello qualunque detto Missaglia*. Few examples of Antonio's work are known. One of these, a plain suit made for the Neapolitan Count Cajazzo about 1480, is in the Vienna Imperial collections. The breast and back plates are not articulated, the pauldrons and tuilles are large and massive, coudières elegant, only the right gauntlet fingered, the leg-pieces with few articulations, and the suit, as so often seen in illustrations, is minus the sollerets. The head-piece is a sallad singularly painted in oils with the Count's armorial bearings, reminding us of the beautifully painted armour of Pisano's St. George published by the Arundel Society, which must have been executed prior to 1450. A jousting suit by him of much later date is engraved and partly gilded, apparently made in 1498 for an envoy of Ludovico Moro to the Emperor Maximilian.

Italian Gothic armour is very much rarer than German. Thoroughness is a German characteristic, and once embarked on a given course the German pursues it until, as is so apparent in their general iron-work, the result becomes exaggeration verging on the grotesque. The Missaglias introduced a certain grace of line into Milanese armour, and the German armourers pursued this vein, making the figures erect and slender and imbuing the waist and bust with womanly elegance. The Italians probably kept to much the same lines, for most representations of armour towards the third quarter of the fifteenth century display the same graceful characteristics, brought to a pitch, however, but little consonant with the stern realities of war, and brusquely set aside before the close of this century.

One of the most formidable of Missaglia's competitors north of the Alps was Hans Grünewalt, born about 1440 and died 1503, regarded by Böheim as one of the foremost armourers of his day. The founder of the bells of St. Sebaldus in 1396, Heinrich Grünewalt, appears to have been the grandfather of a family which became considerable in Nuremberg, building the still standing Pilatus House, properly the "Zum geharnischten Mann." Hans was employed by Maximilian when King of the Romans, and no armourer in Germany was more sought after. While he flourished Nuremberg was the most renowned of any city of Germany for the production of armour, but on his death Augsburg was allowed to entirely supplant it.

The Colman family migrated from Bâle to Augsburg about 1377, to again quote from Böheim. Georg, the father of Lorenz, was well established as an armourer when he was joined in 1467 by his famous son. In 1477 they were honoured with a commission from Maximilian, then King of the Romans, for a complete harness for horse and man, which was executed to his entire satisfaction. Georg died two years later. In 1490 Lorenz was appointed Court Armourer, and he had prospered so far as to be able to afford pecuniary assistance to the ever-needy Maximilian. Towards 1506 he worked for the Court of Mantua, receiving through the house of Fugger a payment of no less than 4000 florins for a harness which gave such satisfaction that a further sum was sent him as a present. In 1507 Maximilian again employed him, and in 1508 begged him to repair personally to Court, when probably the important change in the fashion of armour, resulting in the Maximilian fluted armour, was devised personally between Lorenz and himself. The first edition of Hans Burgkmair's woodcut engraving of the Emperor in a full suit of this armour for horse and man appeared in this same year. Lorenz died in 1516. The only authentic suits by him known to Böheim are in the Imperial collections of Vienna. One is the magnificent Gothic suit made in 1493 for Maximilian, a far more complete and defensive suit than those we have figured, but with similar fleur-de-lis pattern engrailing to the margins of the plates, while some of the upper edges on the limb pieces are rolled over and finished with a cable border. The suit is graceful and of exquisite workmanship, slightly fluted in the arms, with fingered gauntlets and moderately long and pointed sollerets. Three other tilting suits bear the Colman mark, the close-helmet surmounted by a cross, with the Augsburg badge and guild mark.

Fig. 10.—German late Gothic Suit. Collection of Mr. Morgan Williams.

The Germans, however, as a race were not all lithe and supple men, and the burly high-living barons could not follow, and hence must have detested the elegancies of Gothic armour. They soon affected an opposite extreme, the clumsy sturdiness seen in so many of the portrait statues of the contemporaries of Maximilian round his cenotaph in Innsbrück. Fig. 10 represents a complete and characteristic suit of this kind belonging to Mr. Morgan Williams. It greatly resembles one figured by Boheim, made for Count Andreas von Sonnenberg about 1508, by Koloman Colman, and now in Vienna. Our suit, preserved in a Rhenish Castle, bears evidence, however, of being considerably earlier, and is regarded by its owner as of about 1495. It is perfectly plain except for some slight fluting on the mittened gauntlets, made to look as if fingered, and on the square-toed sollerets. The tuilles are still an important feature, but wide and plain. Some German suits of this date look affectedly ungainly; such as a mounted suit attributed to Duke John of Saxony, which is slightly fluted and bears the great tilting helm.

Fig. 11.—Suit of Maximilian Fluted Armour. Belonging to Mr. Percy Macquoid.

The Maximilian fluted armour is a development of this, belonging, however, rather to Renaissance than Gothic times. With its introduction the elegance so distinctive of late Gothic armour passed definitely out of fashion and gave place to armour in which the opposite characteristics were sought. The flutings which invest the Maximilian suits with so much character must have been suggested more or less by the shell-like ridgings and flutes of Gothic armour. The leading idea was the substitution of a stiff unyielding defence for one that was supple and pliable. The articulations of the breast and back plates—except in rare instances, such as the magnificent Nuremberg suit formerly worn by Lord Stafford, in which the breast-plate was formed of two pieces and decorated with graceful open-work tracery—were wholly abolished, and replaced by a stout and rigid pectoral more adapted to receive the shock of the lance in the tilt-yard. The form of tourney had changed, and was now chiefly tilting with a light and hollow lance, calculated to shiver at the impact, as may be seen in specimens still preserved in the Tower. The pliable Gothic suits adapted for mixed tourneys and for actual warfare were out of place in the tilt as now practised; and the heavy man-at-arms in full cap-à-pie armour had ceased to play the preponderating part in war and was shortly destined to disappear from the field. No longer was his function, as hitherto, to engage in the melée, and bear the brunt of the battle: this was sustained by the pike, arquebus, light-armed cavalry and artillery; the heavy-armed cavalry being reserved for charges in which the weight of man and horse sheathed in steel might ride down the opposing force.

Plate VI.—Casque of an Officer of the Guard of Cosmo de' Medici. Collection of Mr. David Currie.

Fig. 12.—Maximilian Armour from Eaton Hall. In the possession of the Duke of Westminster, K.G.

All the cap-à-pie suits of fluted Maximilian armour resemble each other in their more salient characteristics. They are extremely defensive and well made, with every piece more or less fluted, except the greaves, which are usually perfectly plain. Many of the pieces have turned-over edges worked into cable patterns. The pauldrons and coudières are well developed, the gauntlets mittened, sollerets with very broad and square toes, breast-plate generally globose, but sometimes brought to a blunt point, often with a roundel guarding the left arm-pit. The armet has usually a low central cabled comb with parallel flutes on either side, occasionally there are three or five combs. The visor is usually thrown into three or four horizontal peaks or ridges, often with the underhung look believed to have been introduced in compliment to the House of Hapsburgh. An almost equally common form is the puffed visor, but the form of the head-piece is generally more varied than that of the rest of the suit. The fine Nuremberg suit, Fig. 11, owned by Mr. Percy Macquoid, shows the bellows visor and the rope crest, and in it all the leading characteristics of Maximilian armour are well displayed, especially the duck-bill sollerets, the flutings of which boldly finish in ram's horns. The suit formerly belonged to the King of Prussia, and seems to be perfect, except the collar, an apparent restoration.

Fig. 13.—Engraved Maximilian Breast-plate. Burges Collection in the British Museum.

Fig. 14.—Portrait. By Piero di Cosimo. National Gallery.

Maximilian armour is greatly favoured by collectors. There are cap-à-pie and barded suits in the Tower and the Wallace collections, at Warwick, and in the collections of Mr. Panmure Gordon and Sir Wheatman Pearson. The horse armour, which nearly entirely sheathes the head, neck, and fore- and hind-quarters, is fluted, gracefully curved, and except the crinière, worked in large pieces, the lower margins curving well away from the flanks. Three-quarter and half suits are well represented in the Tower and the Wallace collections, the one figured, Fig. 12, being a finely typical example brought from Strawberry Hill, and now the property of the Duke of Westminster. This armour seems to have been at times partly gilded, and instances exist where small badges are repeated to form bands of raised work between the flutes. It is sometimes engraved with borders of floral design, either edging the different pieces, or more boldly treated as in Fig. 13 from the Burges Collection in the British Museum. Though mainly worn in Germany, fluted armour became everywhere the fashion, the portrait by Piero di Cosimo, Fig. 14, in the National Gallery affording an admirable representation of a breast-plate with delicate flutes on the lower half. An actual specimen resembling this, but engraved, is in the collection from Rhodes at Woolwich. The corselets furnished to the Swiss pike-men by the Milanese appear also to have been of this pattern. Besides the bellows visor, and one puffed out to give breathing space and fluted, the visor was at times embossed into the form of a grotesque face with mustachios. Sometimes the helmets in which this occurs had a pair of fan-like appendages in pierced and fluted steel, forming a dignified and wing-like crest. The remarkable example in the Tower, Fig. 15, once silvered, and presented by Maximilian himself to Henry VIII., has a pair of ram's horns instead of wings. It has since been painted and rendered more absurd by spectacles, and assigned without any reason to the King's jester, Will Somers.

Fig. 15.—Helmet. Presented by Maximilian to Henry VIII. Tower of London.

These grotesque helmets were sometimes worn with armour puffed and slashed to imitate civilian dress. A few pieces of this kind are in the Tower, but the Wallace Collection possesses a three-quarter suit, slashed, puffed, engraved, and gilt, the armet having the bellows visor and five-roped comb. The extreme of exaggeration to which German armourers were carried is seen in the suit in the Ambras Collection, figured by Hefner and by Hewett, in which the cloth bases as well as the puffed sleeves of the civilian are carefully imitated in steel. The visor is singularly grotesque, and the whole presents a ludicrous and ungainly appearance, as well as being quite unserviceable.

Fig. 16.—Cap-à-pie Suit of Henry VIII., on a Horse barded with Embossed Burgundian Armour of the time of Henry VII. Tower of London.

The cap-à-pie suit of Henry VIII., Fig. 16, belongs to this group, and though not fluted, is made like the Maximilian armour, the high erect shoulder-piece and large coudières giving it a striking character. The armet is of fine form, with the visor thrown into the series of peaks and ridges common to fluted armour, and known to collectors as the bellows shape. The bridle-hand wears the mainfere (main-de-fer), while the right hand grasping the spear is gauntleted. The horse armour, though so boldly embossed, is of earlier date, not later than Henry VII. The foliated scrolls surround the *cross ragulé* and steel brickets and fire-stones, so that it probably presents a rare specimen of the Burgundian armourer's craft.

Fig. 17.—Tilting Helm. Time of Henry VII. Westminster Abbey.

The head-piece for tilting used in Germany and England during the reign of Henry VII. and first years of Henry VIII., and known a century earlier, is represented, Fig. 17, by the remarkably perfect specimen found in the triforium of Westminster Abbey in 1869. It weighs 17½ lbs., the few others known in England weighing, with one exception, considerably over 20 lbs. When fixed, the helm itself was immovable, but as there were quite three inches of space round the head, movement inside was possible. The occularium is placed so that the head must be lowered to see out, the combatants sighting each other like bulls before making their rush, and throwing up the head to escape splinters of the lance.

The abandonment of this heavy helm for a much lighter form may have been due to Henry VIII. himself. Hall narrates that tilting on one occasion in 1524, with his great friend and brother-in-law Brandon, Duke of Suffolk, he had on a helmet of a new fashion, devised by himself, the like of which had not before been seen. It had a visor, which was up and unfastened, leaving the king's face exposed, when by some mischance the word was given to Brandon to start. No doubt in the old helm, and remarking that he could not see, he couched his lance, striking the king on the brow of the skull-piece or main portion of his helmet. Appalled at the narrow escape, he vowed he would never tilt with his sovereign more. One of the lighter forms of tilting helmet, Fig. 18, from Penshurst, shows the small trapdoor for speaking or breathing, but now riveted down. A second helmet, Fig. 19, of rather later date, is surmounted by the porcupine crest in wood, removed in the illustration, and is interesting as having belonged to the grandfather of Sir Philip Sidney. Both these helmets perhaps hung in Penshurst Church.

Fig. 18.—Tilting Helmet. Early sixteenth century. At Penshurst.

Fig. 19.—Tilting Helmet of an Ancestor of Sir Philip Sidney. Penshurst.

The sallad, the head-piece *par excellence* of Gothic armour, continued in use, especially in Germany, until far into the sixteenth century. In its simplest form it was the archer's head-piece: but provided with slits for vision, pulled over the brow in time of danger to meet the chin defence or bavier, it became almost a closed helmet; and with the further addition of a visor and other reinforcing pieces, it was used for battle or tilting by the mounted knight. It was never a very safe head-piece, De Commines relating how the Count of Charolois received a sword-wound on the neck at Montlhéry, 1465, for want of his bavier, "which, being slightly fastened in the morning, dropped from his head in the battle—I myself saw it fall." The Venetian form survived during the seventeenth century, though for pageantry rather than use, being covered with red velvet richly ornamented with beaten iron foliage and scrolls, gilded and sometimes surmounted by a swan-like crest. The richness of decoration of the sallad has been alluded to in the former monograph. The battle picture by Paolo Uccello, Fig. 8, shows one covered with red velvet and studded with nails. Elizabeth with her own hands garnished the sallad of Henry VII. with jewels, and in 1513 Erasmus Kirkener received £462:4:2 for "garnishing a salet" and a head-piece, "and mending a shapewe." Pope Pius V. sent Alva a sallad and sword for his brave fights for the Church. Wooden shields covered with painted canvas, embossed leather, or gesso, continued in use in Germany down to about the end of the reign of Maximilian. The magnificent specimen, Plate I., is now in the British Museum. Of late fifteenth century date, it is of wood lined with leather, faced with canvas, over which a layer of gesso has been laid to receive the gilding. Upon the gold ground the design has been painted, a knight in Gothic armour, with armet and poll-axe on the ground before him, kneeling to a lady, with the appropriate legend *Vous ou la mort*. The surfaces are finely curved. In the Tower inventory, quoted by Lord Dillon, among the jewels is a target of the Passion with Our Lady and St. George.

The splendid decoration of the sword-hilts used with Gothic armour has already been noticed. By the kindness of Sir Noël Paton an exquisite specimen in the finest preservation is illustrated in Fig. 20. The pommel and cross-hilt are plated with silver gilt, and the former bears a shield with the arms of Battle Abbey and the initials T. L. of Abbot Thomas de Lodelowe, 1417-1434. It came into the possession of Sir John Gage, K.G., on the suppression of the monasteries, his descendant presenting it to the Meyrick Collection. Few existing swords, except those used as municipal insignia, are in equal preservation, but richly worked hilts are represented in brasses and monuments. Swords abounded in churches, but few are left besides the royal swords at Westminster, Canterbury, and Windsor. Part of the glamour surrounding Joan of Arc was due to the consecrated sword taken by her from St. Catherine's Church at Tours. The sword of Guy, Earl of Warwick, was specially mentioned in a will of the time of Henry IV., and its custody confirmed to the family after the accession of Henry VIII. It is curious to note that in 1319 the wearing of swords in London was forbidden, and those confiscated were hung up beneath Ludgate, within and without.

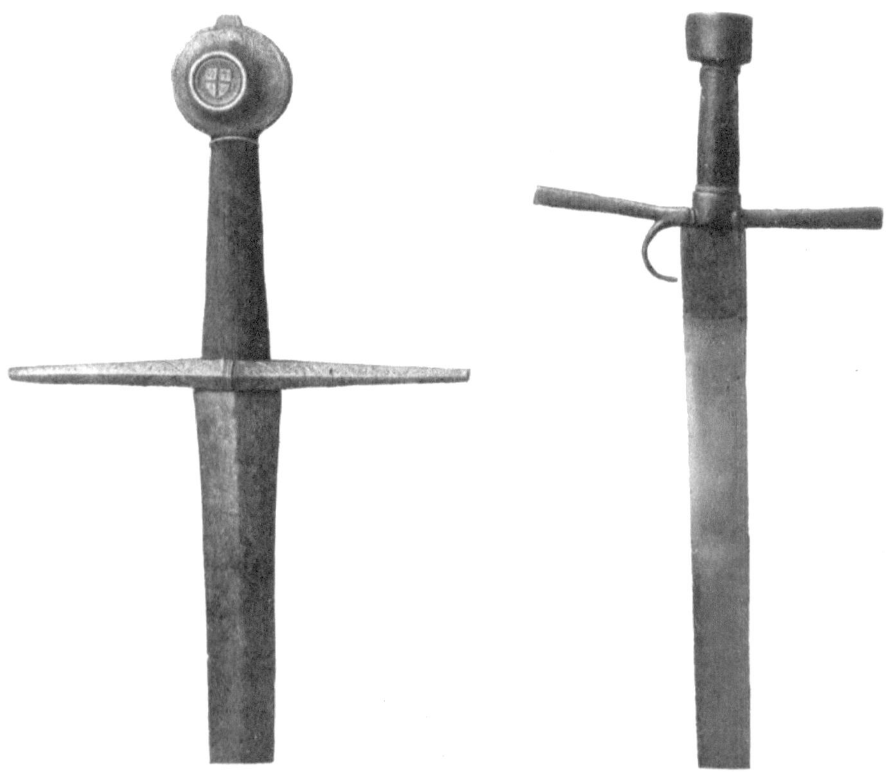

Fig. 20.—The Sword of Battle Abbey.
Fifteenth century. Collection of Sir
Noël Paton.

Fig. 21.—Sword of 14th century, with
Guard for Forefinger. Windsor Castle.

The interesting sword, Fig. 21, from Her Majesty's collection at Windsor, dates from about the end of the fourteenth or early in the fifteenth century. Its peculiarity is the semicircular guard for the forefinger growing out of one of the quillons, the first step, as Baron de Cosson remarks, "towards the evolution of the beautiful and complicated rapier of the sixteenth century." "The pommel and guard are of iron fully gilt, the grip of wood." The blade is gilt and engraved for a few inches where it shows dark in the illustration, and is inscribed with the name of the Cid Marchio Rodericus Bivar and a shield of arms, these having been added, in the Baron's opinion, in the sixteenth or seventeenth century. Only four swords with the little semicircular guard or "half pas d'ane" were known when he described them, being introduced owing to the Italian custom of bending the forefinger round the quillon when slashing.

CHAPTER IV
ENRICHED ARMOUR

Armour was enriched in almost all ages, sometimes ostentatiously so, and at other times left affectedly plain. It was, however, only when wearing it in battle ceased to be a paramount necessity, that armour definitely became little more than a mere vehicle for lavish display. Lightly armed and easily manœuvred troops and artillery were steadily becoming increasingly important factors in deciding the fortunes of battle, and at last men could with difficulty be brought to undergo the fatigue of carrying weighty armour which they regarded as no efficient protection. Sir James Smith's complaint in 1530 puts the matter clearly: "But that which is more strange, these our new fantasied men of warre doo despise and scorne our auncient arming of ourselves, both on horseback and on foot, saying that wee armed ourselves in times past with too much armour, or peeces of yron (as they terme it). And therefore their footmen piqueurs they do allow for very well armed when they weare their burgonets, their collars, their cuirasses, and their backs, without either pouldrons, vambraces, gauntlets, or tasses." This arming is even lighter than Mr. J. F. Sullivan's picturesque Marauder of Picardie (Plate II.). The Battle of the Spurs perhaps did much to break the prestige of men-at-arms, who were routed by one-tenth their number of English horse. The French chivalry, armed cap-à-pie, came on in three ranks thirty-six deep, and were targets as usual for the English archers, who lined a hedge, "and shotte apace and galled the French horse." The English horse, and a few mounted archers who had gone forward with spears, "set on freshly crying St. George," whereupon the French fled, throwing away "speres, swordes, and mases," and cutting the bards of their horses. The Estradiots coming down in front of the French host caught sight of the English horse, and mistaking the king's battaille of foot for horse also, turned and fled, chased by the Burgundians and Walloons; the main body of English, on foot with the king, having no opportunity of engaging.

The large proportion of mercenaries retained on either side contributed more perhaps than anything else to the disuse of armour. Nicander Nucius relates that in Henry VII.'s expedition to Scotland there were "Italians in no small number, and of Spaniards, and also moreover of Argives from Peloponnesus." In 1546 Lord Grey de Wilton brought his "Bullenoyes and Italian harquebuziers" from Boulogne. In invading Scotland two years later he divided "his menne of armes, demilaunces, and light horsemenne into troops, appointing the Spanish and Italian hagbutters on horsebacke to keepe on a wing." Captain Gambo, a Spaniard, and others held command, and, "being backed by the Almayne footmen, entered againe into Scotland."

Fig. 22.—German Armour. Date about 1570. The Duke of Westminster, K.G.

In proceeding to quell the insurrection in Devonshire, Lord Grey's forces included, among other strangers, a band of horsemen "most part Albanoyses and Italians," and a band of Italian footmen under Captain Paule Baptist Spinola of Genoa. These mercenaries armed themselves in their own fashion and were not to be controlled. Nor does it appear that the Tudor kings were anxious to put even their body-guards in anything like complete armour. Henry VII.'s guard consisted "of fifty yeomen, tall personable men, good archers, and divers others." A little later, on the marriage of Prince Arthur, the guard consisted of 300 carrying halberts, in white and green damask, with garlands of vine embroidered back and front, richly spangled in front and enclosing a red rose worked in bullion and goldsmith's work. Nicander Nucius says that "they consisted of halberdmen and swordsmen who used bucklers and Italian swords, so that resting the bucklers on the ground, they could discharge arrows." Perkin Warbeck, posing as the "Whyte Rose Prince of England," had a guard of thirty in "Murray and blewe." Henry VIII. appointed a guard of fifty "speeres" in the first year of his reign, each to be attended by an archer, demilaunce, and a custrell, on great horses. They were so extravagantly dressed, "trapped in cloth of golde, silver, and goldsmithes woorke, and their servants richly appareled also," that "they endured not long the apparell and charges were so greate." They were not reinstated until the thirty-first year of his reign. Edward VI.'s guard was 400 strong, all very tall, and dressed in crimson velvet doublets embroidered with golden roses. In meeting Philip of Spain on his way to Winchester in 1554, Lord Arundel took 100 archers in yellow cloth striped with red velvet with their bows ready, Mary's colours, however, being white and green.

The taste for sumptuous armour became definitely fixed on the accession of Henry VIII. in 1509. Harding relates that, at the Coronation jousts, Brandon "turneyed in harneyes all over gylte from the heade-peece to the Sabattons." Hall devotes scores of pages to descriptions of the magnificence of Henry, especially in presence of rival potentates or their ambassadors. Before Terouenne, the weather being very foul, Maximilian and his retinue came to the rendezvous in black cloth, but Henry was attended by a large retinue extravagantly dressed, comprising his usual "nine henxmen" in white and crimson cloth of gold richly embroidered with goldsmith's work, on great coursers as richly caparisoned, with the addition of many gold bells, and "tassels of fyne gold in bullion"—these bore his helm; "the two grangardes," his spears, axe, etc. He entered Terouenne as a conqueror in "armure gilt and graven"; and Maximilian set out on his return "toward Almaine in gilte harness, and his nobles in white harness and rich cotes." On the occasion of the French ambassador's visit to Greenwich, the king disported himself at the "tilte in a newe harnesse all gilte of a strange fashion that had not been seen." No less than 286 spears were broken. Charles V. is often represented in very richly embossed armour, and some of the suits made for him, such as by the Colmans of Augsburg, show that these sculptured and pictorial representations were not wholly imaginary.

It is not, however, until the reigns of Mary and Elizabeth that the culminating point of richness in armour is attained, when poems abound in allusions to it. In Spenser's *Faerie Queen* armour always glitters with gold, and in Camoens' *Lusiad* there are "breast-plates flaming with a thousand dyes."

Little sumptuously decorated armour was made in England, the finest that can claim to have been made here being five existing suits out of the twenty-nine in the Jacobe album. One only of these belongs to the nation, Lord Bucarte's bequeathed with the Wallace Collection; the opportunity of acquiring Sir Christopher Hatton's, notwithstanding its historic interest, being hitherto neglected.

Fig. 23.—Suit of late Italian Armour. Embossed and damascened. Tower of London.

Of foreign armour the suits of the Dukes of Bourbon and Montmorency at Wilton are spoils of victory, and others in the Tower and at Windsor were royal presents. The vast bulk of foreign armour in the country, however, has been acquired by purchase, and of late years. Of small collections one of the least known is that made by the grandfather of the Duke of Westminster, who purchased it from Sir Horace Walpole. The light peascod breast-plate and tassets (Fig. 22), richly engraved and gilt in bands, are probably German of about 1570, and the gauntlets of approximately the same date, while the close helmet is about twenty years earlier. The finely engraved and parcel-gilt breast-plate and tassets (Plate III.) are probably Italian, dating from about 1540. A deep peascod breast-plate and tassets richly arabesqued with dolphins on a blue ground, bears an engraved escutcheon with the figure of a porcupine, motto and date.

Fig. 24.—Fine Italian Breast-plate, c. 1550. Said to have been worn by Philip of Spain. Collection of Mr. David Currie.

One of the most sumptuously decorated suits in the Tower, for long described as that of the Black Prince, is reproduced in Fig. 23. It is late Italian, much of it embossed with lions' heads, etc., while the plainer surfaces are entirely covered with very delicate gold ornament on russet ground. Detail of the damascening is shown in Plate IV.

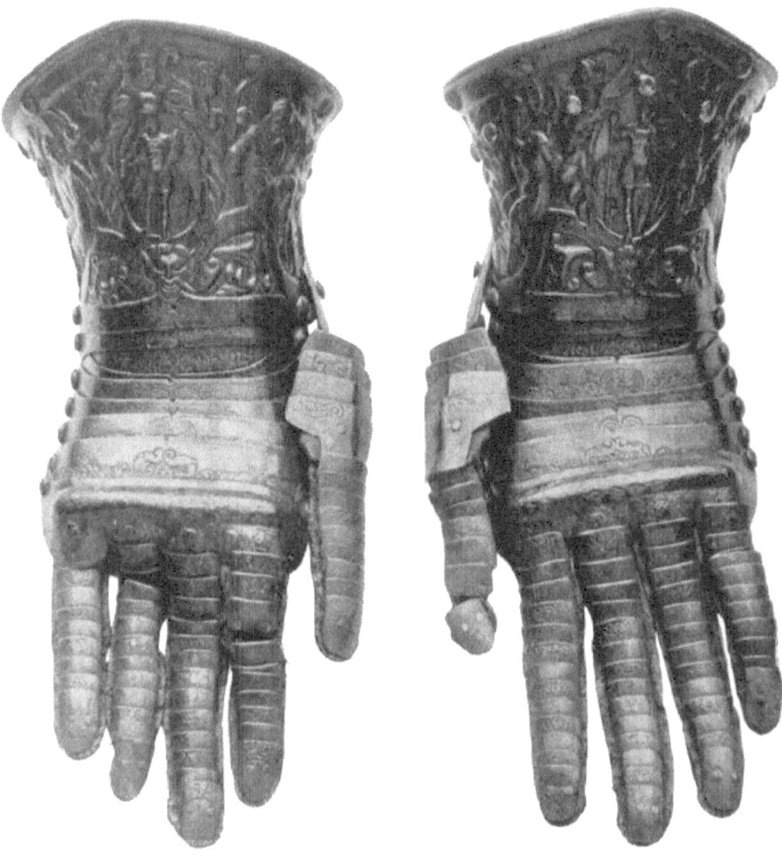

Fig. 25.—Pair of fine Italian Gauntlets. Possibly belonging to the same Suit as the Breast-plate. Collection of Mr. David Currie.

Several of our illustrations are taken from Mr. David Currie's magnificent collection, part of which is deposited in the South Kensington Museum. Very little armour is finer in its way than the breast-plate (Fig. 24) formerly in the Bernal and Londesborough collections. The repoussé work, designed in the best Italian taste of the sixteenth century, is enhanced by gold damascening on backgrounds gilt and inlaid with silver. It is said to have been worn by Philip of Spain, the steel gauntlets (Fig. 25), of similar work, having perhaps formed part of the same suit. It recalls one in Madrid presented to the Infant Philip III. by the Duke of Terranova. The finely embossed breast-plate (Plate V.), and gorget (Fig. 26), are French, but unfortunately no history attaches to them.

Fig. 26.—Embossed Gorget. French, c. 1550. Collection of Mr. David Currie.

Fig. 27.—Silver Armour of Prince Charles, afterwards Charles II. Tower of London.

This extremely costly armour, with no defensive quality, was intended for parade rather than use, and an appropriate head-piece was also especially devised for triumphal display. This was the casque, based on classic models, which left the face entirely uncovered. Artists of high renown, like Verrocchio and Pollajuolo, designed and worked upon these *casques d'honneur*, and the Negrolis, Colmans, and other famous armourers vied with each other in their production. Superb examples exist in the great national collections of Europe, but rarely find their way into private hands. Plate VI., not one of the finest examples, was formerly in Lord Londesborough's, and now in Mr. Currie's collection. It has a triple comb and plume-holder, and is believed to have formed part of the armour of an officer of the guard to Cosmo de' Medici.

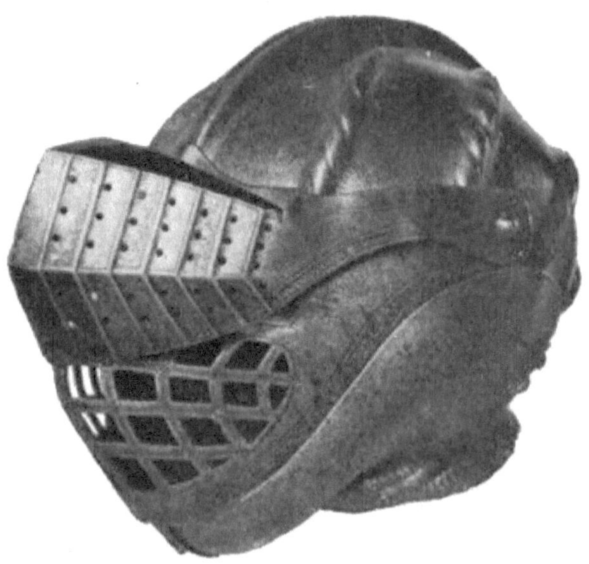

Fig. 28.—Sixteenth century Armet of rare form, with double visor. Mr. E. Cozens Smith.

The casque passes almost insensibly into the more serviceable burgonet, a classic-looking helmet with ear-pieces and neck-covering, dear to Salvator Rosa and his contemporaries. This developed into the spider helmet with bars to protect the face, and the open and barred helmets of Charles I. and the Commonwealth. Fig. 27 represents an extremely rich example of the latter, made with cuirass and gorget in repoussé silver for Charles II. when prince. The defensive quality of the armet, not being so purely consecrated to parade, was rarely impaired by embossing, and even when made for monarchs, the decoration was mainly confined to etching and gilding. A rare form with double visor, five rope-like combs, and bands of engraving, is illustrated (Fig. 28) from the collection of Mr. Cozens Smith of Benyeo. The armet continued to be used by mounted officers until the middle of the seventeenth century, a picture of Rocroy, 1643, showing Condé in a hat, but his staff in visored helmets. One of the latest cap-à-pie suits, probably never worn, is that in the Tower, richly worked and gilded all over, presented to Charles I. by the City of London.

Fig. 29.—Suit of parcel-gilt Armour. Made for Prince Charles, afterwards
Charles I. Tower of London.

The high-combed morions and cabassets of the pikemen and musketeers are
generally richly etched in vertical bands, or covered with interlacing arabesques,
which we gather, from numerous passages in Brantôme's works, were usually gilt.
Thus 4000 harquebuziers stepped out of the ranks as *enfans perdus*, at the call of

Mons. d'Andelet "tous morions gravez et dorez en teste."

**Fig. 30.—Richly Embossed and Damascened Target. Italian, sixteenth century.
Mr. David Currie's Collection.**

The buckler or target appears an archaic defence, but survived with us, sometimes in high favour like the sword, at others nearly obsolete, until the reign of James I., and in Scotland till recent times. It was banished while the Spanish rapier and left-handed dagger were in use.

Plate VII.—Lower part of enriched Chanfron. Suit presented to Charles I. by the City of London. Tower of London.

The most magnificent targets were made solely for parade, and were borne in front of princely personages by their esquires. The broad surfaces they presented for decoration, and the esteem they were held in, induced even very great artists, like Giulio Romano, not only to design them, but actually to work upon them. It is far from rare to find in collections of drawings by old masters, designs for shields, like those signed Polydore and B. Franco hanging in the corridors at Chatsworth. Under the Tudor and later Valois kings they were usually round and of steel, but sometimes elliptical, obovate, vesica-shaped, rectangular, and even heater-shaped, with painted arms. One of the finest ever produced is the Milanese buckler at Windsor, believed to have been in England since the time of Francis I. The repoussé work is of most exquisite finish and the gold damascening of extraordinary delicacy. Others not inferior to it are at Dresden, Turin, and Madrid, the latter by Colman of Augsburg. The shield of Charles IX. in the Louvre is also superbly damascened. Magnificent specimens are known from the hands of the Negrolis and Picinino of Milan, Gasparo Mola of Florence, Giorgio Ghisi of Mantua. A description of one, now lost, by Hieronymus Spacini of Milan, states that it comprised forty-eight engravings in gold upon niello. Hans Mielich has left several designs, some of which were carried out by Colman. The finely-embossed target in the Kensington Museum is signed by Georgius Sigman of Augsburg. The Bernal, Meyrick, Soltykoff, and other collections now dispersed, included examples illustrating the story of Coriolanus, Siege of Troy, Judgment of Paris, etc.

Fig. 31.—Target of Etched Steel. Italian or German, about 1550. Mr. P. Davidson's Collection.

Those intended to receive the hard knocks of active service must have presented unembossed surfaces, though perhaps richly etched and gilded like the morions. The specimen (Fig. 30) belonging to Mr. Currie is rich enough for parade, with its bands of embossing and fine damascening, while the second illustration (Fig. 31) might have been the war target of an Italian or Spanish Captain under Philip II. It is remarkable that the first Greenwich inventory only contains eight bucklers, "of steele, seven guilte and wroughte." They were probably somewhat like Fig. 31. Another among the jewels was of silver gilt, with the arms of England, roses, castles, and pomegranates. This, like the quaint little roundel belonging to Lord Kenyon (Fig. 32), was probably English. It appears that London bucklers acquired some celebrity in the time of Elizabeth, who limited the length of their steel points to two inches, for the young King of Scots greatly desired to possess one. George Brownfelde, Roger Morgan, Tothill Street, and Richard Hamkyn, King Street, Westminster, were buckler-makers to Henry VIII.; and Peter Lovat, a Frenchman, supplied steel pavices at the sign of the cock in Fleet Street at eight shillings each. They are seldom mentioned as playing a part in actual warfare, though when Lord Grey de Wilton called for forlorn hopes at the siege of Guynes, fifty stept out "with swordes and roondelles to view and essaye the breatches." The celebrated Jarnac duel, witnessed by Henri II., was fought with sword and target.

Fig. 32.—Roundel with National Badges and Inscription. Belonging to Lord Kenyon.

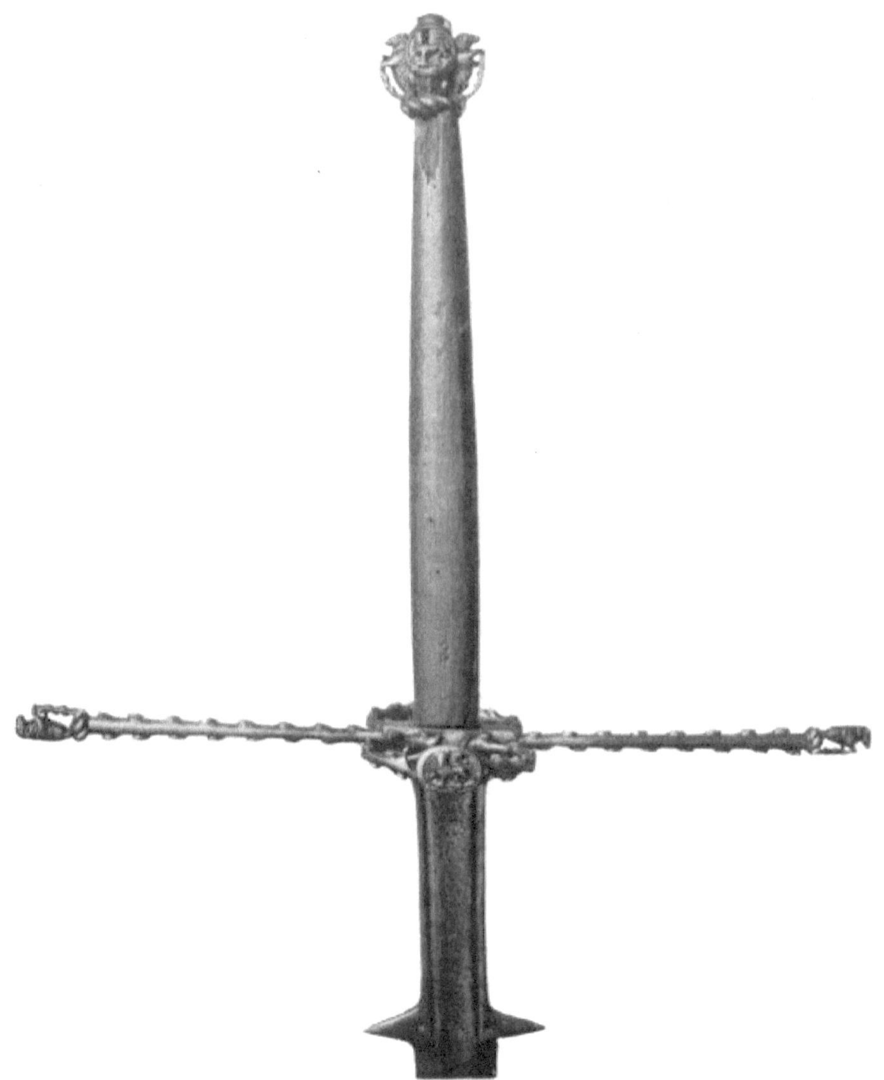

**Fig. 33.—Hilt of Two-handed Sword with the Bear and Ragged Staff on the
Pommel and Quillons in chased steel. Penshurst.**

The chanfron or head-piece to the horse's armour, originally called the chev-
ron, received as much attention as the helmet or buckler of its rider. It was the
pride of the noble, when Monstrelet wrote, to make the horse's head-front blaze
with jewels. Designs for horse-armour by Hans Mielich, and that actually executed
for Christian II. at Dresden, are as rich as the suits themselves. The latter illustrates
the labours of Hercules, and is the one for which Colman received 14,000 crowns.
The chanfron bears a spike, an appendage dating back to the time of Edward III.
In the *Anturs of Arthur* we read—

Opon his chèveronne be-forn
Stode as a unicorn
Als scharpe as a thorn,
An nanlas of stele.

The charger ridden by Lord Scales in his tourney with the Bastard of Burgundy had a "schaffrõ with a large sharpe pyke of stele," which, penetrating the nostrils of the Bastard's steed, caused it to rear and throw him. The oldest chanfron handed down is that in Warwick Castle, which was there when visited by Sir William Dugdale. The lower part of one belonging to the suit, Fig. 29, is seen in Plate VII.

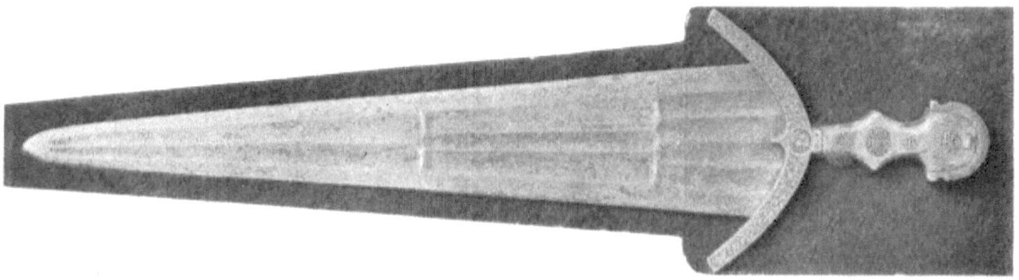

Fig. 34.—Venetian Cinquedea, engraved, with Ivory Handle. The Duke of Norfolk.

Swords varied considerably in the sixteenth century, the extremes sometimes meeting in the same army, the two-handed sword, scimitar, rapier, sabre, cinquedea, falchion, and malchus, being borne perhaps simultaneously by the mercenary bands comprised in it. The two-handed sword represents the largest dimensions ever attained by this weapon, perhaps originating in the sword of state, like that of Edward III. in Westminster Abbey. It was used in Scotland at an early period; if not wielded by whole clans, certainly by champions of exceptional vigour. Thus Froissart relates that Sir Archibald Douglas fought on foot and wielded an immense sword, the blade of which was two ells long, and so heavy that scarcely any other man could have lifted it from the ground. This great sword is the real claymore, though the name has been misappropriated to the Scottish basket-hilted broadsword of the last century. The Swiss and Germans were the only people who made it an offensive weapon for large disciplined bodies of troops, and in the sixteenth century it had become an essentially Teutonic weapon. Henry VIII.'s great personal strength and agility enabled him to wield it, as a young man, and to withstand all-comers. The fine hilt illustrated (Fig. 33) from Penshurst, with the pommel and quillons carved and chased out of the solid steel into the bears and ragged staff of the Leicesters, is undoubtedly the most beautiful in the country. The blade has been shortened, perhaps under the edict of Queen Elizabeth, who posted guards at the City Gates to break all swords that were too long.

Fig. 35.—Main-Gauche with Steel Hilt. Belonging to Mr. Percy Macquoid.

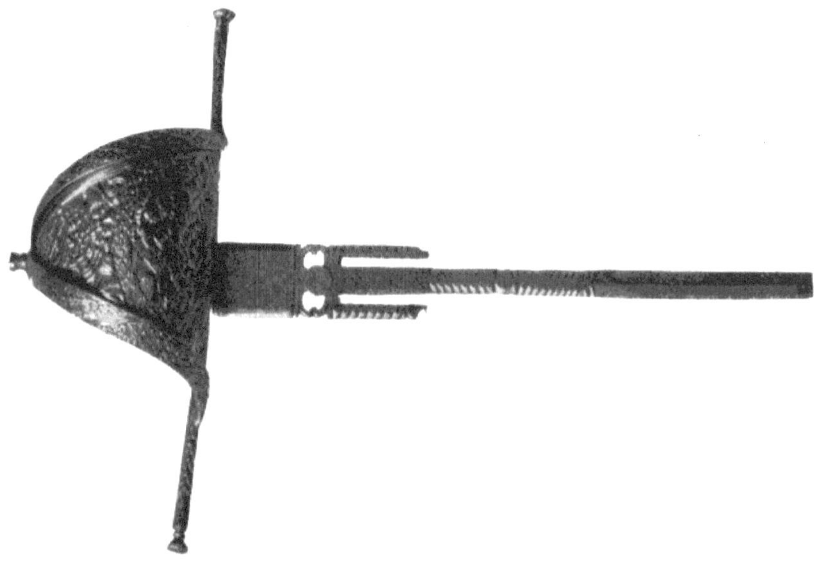

Fig. 36.—Main-Gauche with Silver Guard. Windsor Castle.

Fig. 37.—Rapier with Silver Guard. Windsor Castle.

In striking contrast to this is the well-known Cinquedea, the Italian translation of the French *Sang de dez*. The name of a spear, *langue-de-bœuf*, has been improperly applied to it since the eighteenth century. The handles were frequently ivory with pierced brass insertions, like the illustration (Fig. 34), belonging to the Duke of Norfolk; but the finest examples are of chased steel, exquisitely worked and silvered. The Cinquedea was highly esteemed in Venice.

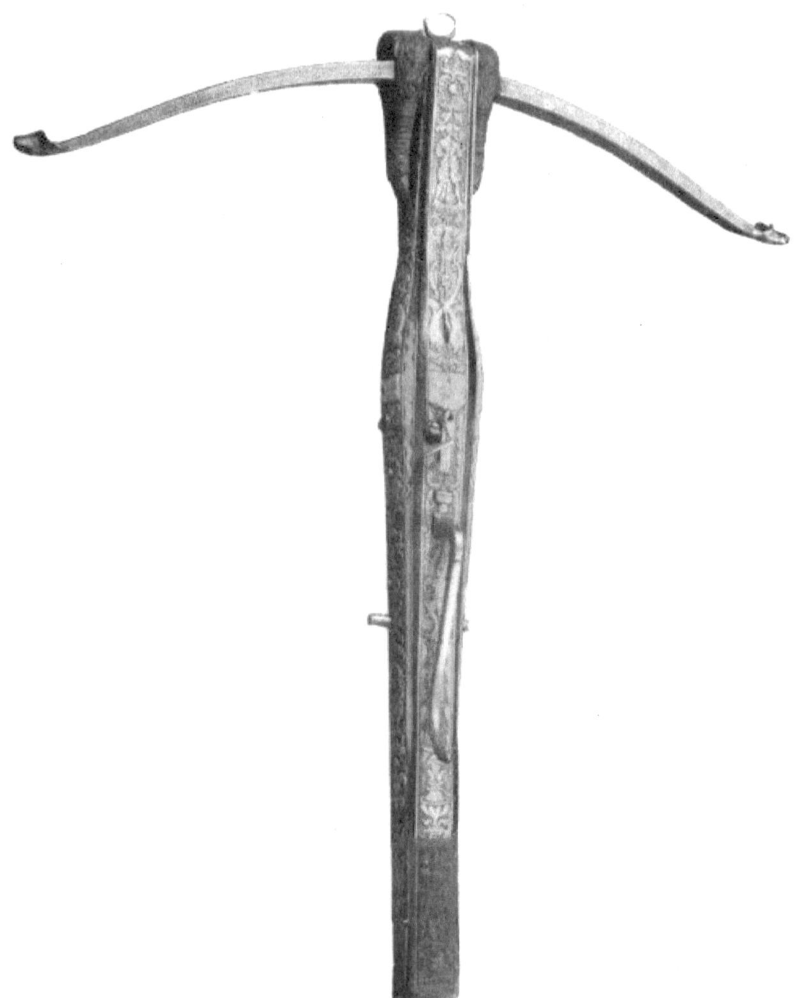

Fig. 38.—Inlaid Ivory Cross-bow. Tower of London.

Until the introduction of the Spanish rapier the sword used with the buckler was short and heavy in the blade, though with handles sometimes richly worked and inlaid with silver. The rapier appeared about 1570 to 1580, the slender tapering blade being relatively of great length, rendering it difficult to sheathe. The guards to the hilts were generally of open work, the variety of form, though endless, falling into three leading groups, the swept-hilted, shell-guard, and cup-hilted, the finest workmanship being as a rule found on the latter. The quillons, generally very long, are either straight or curved. With the rapier, a long dagger held in the left hand and called the *main-gauche* was used to parry, the blade being notched near the base to entangle and break the opponent's weapon. Two varieties are figured, both with superbly chased hilts; the one of steel belonging to Mr. Percy Macquoid (Fig. 35), and one with silver guard (Fig. 36), belonging to Her Majesty. The cup-hilted rapier (Fig. 37), reproduced on a slightly smaller scale, is the companion to the latter dagger and is also partly silver-hilted and chased with representations of combats. The quillons are engraved with flowers, and the blade is signed Heinrich Coell, Solingen. The blades and hilts were frequently, perhaps usually, made in different workshops. Many of those in Vienna have German hilts and Italian blades, others have Solingen blades and Milanese hilts. Toledo blades were, however, preferred, and their marks were frequently imitated by German makers. The first ship of the ill-fated Spanish Armada to fall a prey to Drake and Howard was the *Capitana* of the Andalusian squadron, which among its treasures carried a chest of swords, richly mounted, and intended for presentation to the English Catholic peers. Frequent reference is made in Elizabethan plays to Bilbao and Toledo blades, but more especially to "Foxes," so called from the Nuremberg mark. Certain passages show that these were used with the buckler, in this country at least; and in the engraving of the funeral of Sir Philip Sidney, targets both round and oval are carried.

The staves, bills, pikes, morris-pikes, holy-water sprinklers, etc., played a very important part in war at this period. The halberds and partisans carried by officers of the harquebusiers, royal guards, and officials were the vehicles for an immense amount of decoration, especially throughout the seventeenth century. Albert Dürer, writing from Venice to Pirkheimer, mentions that the Italian lansquenets "have roncoins with 218 points, and if they pink a man with any of these, the man is dead, as they are all poisoned." This could hardly have been serious, but a sheet of drawings by Leonardo da Vinci shows some very extraordinary forms. Most of the varieties of staves were no doubt originally developments of the peasant scythes, bill-hooks, pitch-forks, and the poll-axe; each country preserving some peculiar form. The cross-bow had long ceased to be a military weapon, but was, owing to its silent fire, still in great repute for sport. It was usually inlaid with ivory, engraved, sometimes stained and heightened with pearl. A fine specimen in the Tower is illustrated (Fig. 38).

CHAPTER V

FIREARMS AND GUNLOCKS
BY MAJOR V. A. FARQUHARSON

The actual date of the first employment of portable firearms is uncertain, but representations of them are frequently met with in the illustrated MSS. of the early part of the fifteenth century, their form at first being simply a tube fastened to a wooden stock, and, according to the coloured drawings, the tube was either of brass or iron. The manner of firing was to apply a match by hand to a touch-hole situated on the upper part of the barrel. The first improvement was to drill the touch-hole in the side of the barrel, with the priming held in a pan formed in a projection also on the side of the barrel, which had a cover, moving on a pivot, thus protecting the powder from the wet or wind till the moment of firing, when it was pushed back by hand. This was the general kind of firearm used during the first half of the fifteenth century. For some time after their introduction, hand firearms were viewed with disfavour, and it was considered more or less unfair to employ them, seeing that the Gothic armour worn by the knights had power to re-sist the ordinary weapons of the field, but took no account of the effects of missiles from the clumsy "gonner." That they were in use in 1453 is evident, as the great Talbot, 1st Earl of Shrewsbury, buried at Whitchurch, came to his end from this cause. "Though at first with manfull courage and sore fighting the Earle wanne the entre of their camp, yet at length they compassed him about, and, *shooting him through the thigh with an hand-gonne,* slew his horse and finally killed him lying on the ground, whom they never durst look in the face, while he stood on his feet" (Hollinshed's *Chronicle*). This was at Chatillon, 20th July 1453.

The first lock was apparently a curved piece of metal in the shape of an S and pivoted in the centre, the upper point holding the match, the lower part, which was prolonged like the lever in the cross-bow, by its weight keeping the match from the pan till this lower part was compressed to the stock on firing.

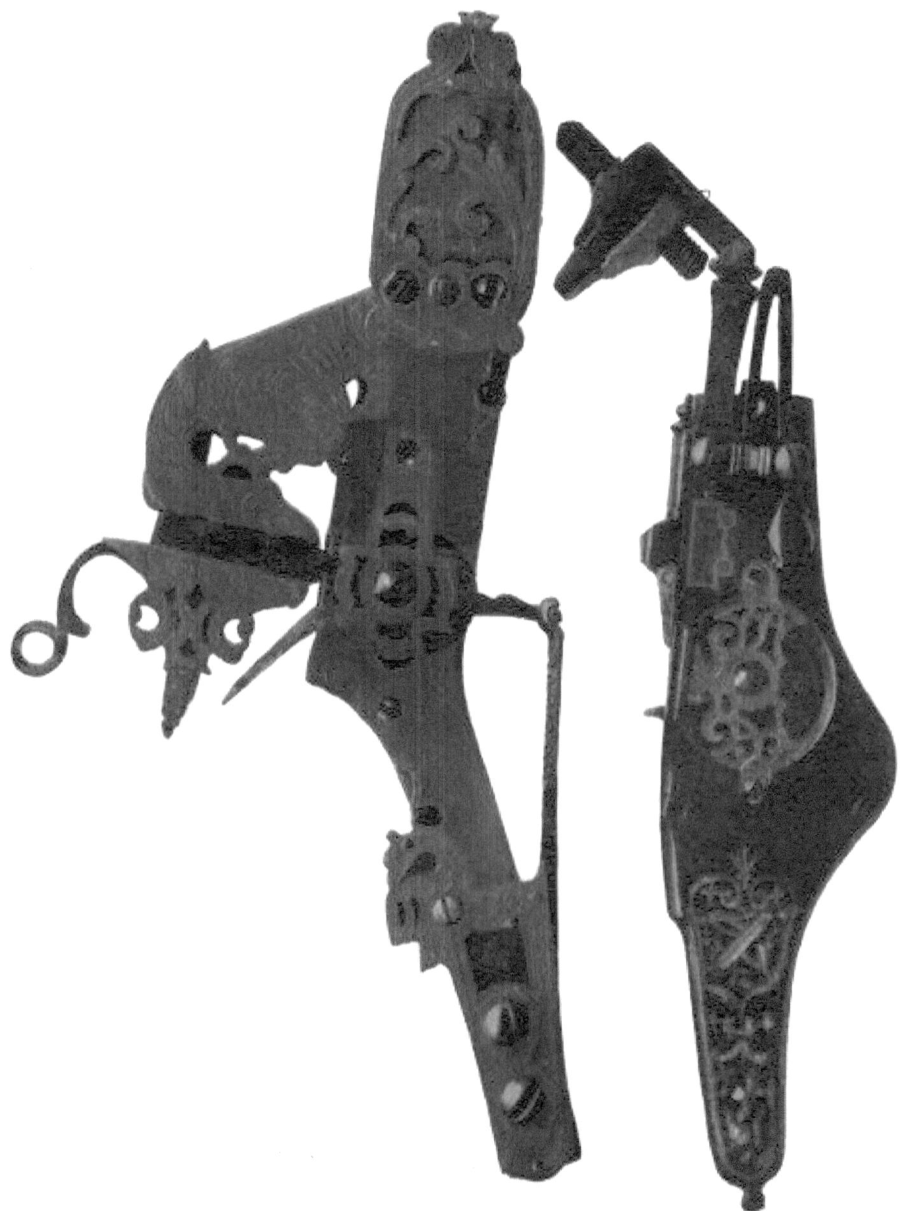

Plate VIII.—Wheel-lock of bright steel, with engraved and pierced brass. German, 17th Century.

Wheel-lock of blued steel, with gold and silver inlay, and wheel-guard of tracery in thin gold. French, 17th Century. Collection of Major Farquharson.

The next stage was the matchlock proper. This is the first lock where the mechanism is complete on a plate. The cock is kept back by a spring acting on the long arm of a lever, while fastened to the short end was a sear or trigger. The pan still projects on the side of the barrel, a principle seen in modern Eastern matchlocks. The next matchlocks had the pan fixed to and forming part of the plate; later matchlocks only vary in the shape of the plate. In the reign of William III. the plates are of the same size as the flint-lock, so that the locks could be changed when required. The matchlock was altogether in use for nearly 200 years, owing to its great simplicity and cheapness. There is a variation of the matchlock in which, by elaborate mechanism, the match is caused to descend on the priming with a snap-action. It is difficult to see the advantage to be obtained from this, as the match it would appear must have broken by contact with the pan, unless it may have taken the form of a stick of hard composition. The head of the match-holders in these locks is a short tube, which gives some probability to this theory, but there is no record to prove it.

The *wheel-lock* is supposed to have been invented in 1517, although a lock belonging to the writer has the date of 1509, yet it is not certain if 1569 is not meant. Nuremberg is reported to be the place of its invention, where indeed, at the time, most things were claimed to have been invented; and the city mark is constantly met with on early locks. It was an important invention, and, except for the delicacy of its mechanism and great expense of production, it was an efficient lock. It consisted briefly of a steel wheel, having from two to four grooves affixed to an axle which passed through the lock-plate, the edge of the wheel appearing through the bottom of the pan. The outer part of the axle was square for a key to fit on, and the inner had a shoulder or crank, which was connected by a shackle chain of three links to an extremely strong spring. The fire stone (pyrites) was fixed in a holder, screwed to the farther end of the lock-plate. The pan had a sliding cover. To put the lock in action a key or "spanner" was placed on the outer end of the axle, and given a ¾ turn; by this the spring was compressed, and kept at tension by the nose of a sear, connected with the trigger, entering a small hole on the inner surface of the wheel. The pan was then primed, the sliding cover brought over it, and the pyrites holder depressed, bringing the pyrites down on the cover. On pulling the trigger the wheel revolved, its axle shoulder knocked back the pan cover and allowed the grooves to grate sparks from the fire-stone, thus firing the priming. There are numerous variations in the wheel-lock of all dates and of many nationalities. By the shape of the feeds, the number of grooves, and by the internal mechanism, and of course by the ornamentation, a tolerable idea can be got of the date or origin of a piece. It is remarkable that the earliest locks were more complete and had appliances that we fail to find in the later. Thus in Fig. 40, a type of the earliest pistol, the lock possesses a safety catch to prevent premature discharge, also a spring-catch to keep the pan cover back. Those, which would be thought advantages, are not to be found in the two examples in Plate VIII. of later date and finer workmanship. In some cases the wheel winds itself, when the pyrites holder is drawn back, thus dispensing with a key. This principle is such an obvious improvement that it seems strange it was not universally adopted.

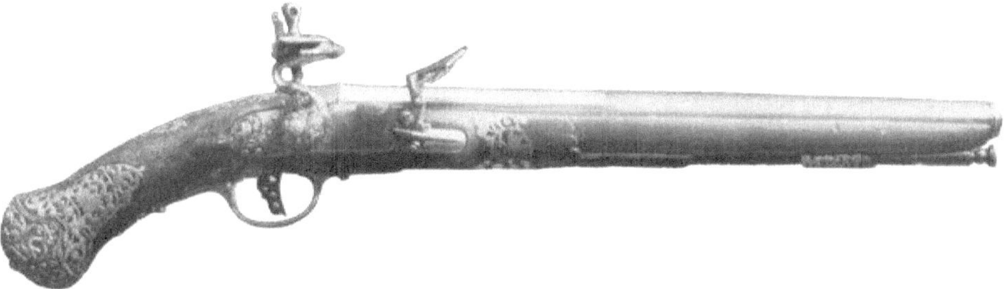

Fig. 39.—Pistol by Lazarino Cominazzo. Collection of Major Farquharson.

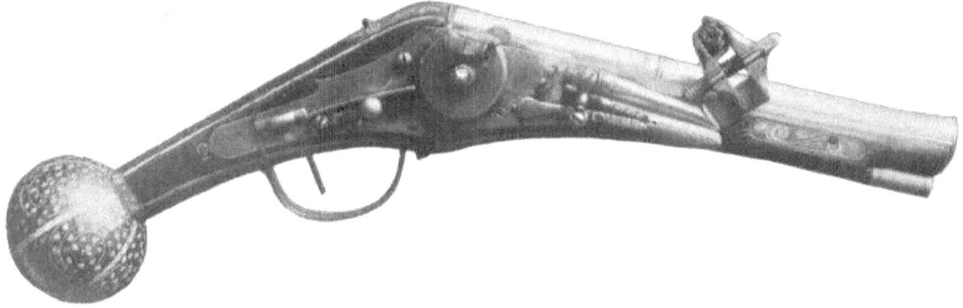

Fig. 40.—Early German Wheel-lock Pistol, used by the Reiters. Collection of Major Farquharson.

A result of the introduction of the wheel-lock was the invention of pistols, which never carry match-locks. The name may have been derived from Pistoia in Tuscany, or, as it has been suggested, from the name of the coin pistole, referring to the bore. There is a word in Italian *pistolese*, but it signifies a knife. Fig. 40 is a good example of an early pistol. It is of the class used by the Reiters, German cavalry, the first body of troops armed with pistols. The barrels at this time are of great thickness, owing to the dread of bursting, and the stocks sloped abruptly, being terminated by a ball butt. This was probably to act as a counterpoise, and also to facilitate drawing the piece from the holster. It would be more efficient, too, when used as a club, as it very frequently was, according to pictures of the time. In early engravings of the Reiter he is armed not only with a pair, but on occasion with four of these pistols, two in the holsters and two fastened to his belt by hasps (Fig. 40 is furnished with a hook or hasp on the reverse side). The Reiter also had a sword. The introduction of the pistol altered the tactics of war; the bodies of horse no longer charged home, but galloped up by ranks, within a few paces of the enemy, discharged their pistols, and then wheeled outward by half troops towards each flank, leaving the front clear for the succeeding rank to take their place. They then reloaded and re-formed ready for another advance. Many of the earlier pistols were wholly of steel. The smaller pistols had a flat butt, cut slanting, and were called Dags. In course of time the barrels were made longer and thinner, the stocks became more straight, and the ball butt elongated, and finally disappeared. The wheel-lock was used for pistols up to 1650. Crusoe, in the Instructions for the

Cavallerie, 1632, gives some fifteen motions for the "firing Exercise" of the wheel pistol.

The Queen possesses a double-barrelled wheel rifle, in which one barrel was placed vertically over the other, dated 1588. It is fired by means of two wheel-locks on one plate, in one of which the works are outside, and the other has them hidden by the plate, the stock is of dark wood, and the fittings of the locks are of chased and gilt metal. Its double barrel, date of the rifling, and the fact of its having a steel ramrod, all make it remarkable. The Dresden arms are on the heel plate, a cypher HF on the stock, and the barrel has a bear as armourer's mark.

The wheel-lock was rarely used for infantry arms, but was of necessity employed by cavalry, where the match was inconvenient.

The next form of lock was the *Snap-hance*, evolved from the wheel-lock by converting the pyrites holder into a fire-steel, and replacing the wheel by a hammer, acted on by a spring and affixed to the opposite side of the pan. The pan and cover remained the same, and the latter slid back as the hammer fell on the steel, leaving the powder bare for the sparks to fall on.

The earliest actual lock of this sort is on a pair of pistols in the Dresden Armoury, dated 1598. The pistols are of the Scotch form, but are probably of Spanish make, as the Highlanders obtained their firearms largely from Spain.

The example Fig. 42 is a snap-hance of Italian make, but of later type (about 1640). It was selected on account of the beautiful chiselled steel of which it is composed. This is in three degrees of relief. The hammer has two dragons entwined on it, and the plate and fire-steel are very richly fashioned, having the armourer's signature on it, GIOVANNI · VATE · BORGOGNONE · IN · BRESCIA. Part of the fire-steel is missing.

The most famous makers of firearms of the middle of the seventeenth century lived in Brescia, such as Lazarino Cominazzo, father and son, Lazaro Lazarino, Francino, and others. Their weapons were famed for extreme lightness and beauty of decoration.

Fig. 39 is a late example of Cominazzo's work. The barrel has a beautiful fluted twist on it, and the lock-plate and hammer, as well as the butt, are chiselled in high relief. These armourers made weapons with each class of lock. It was quite the thing for any one on their grand tour to visit Brescia, and bring back one of these famed weapons. Evelyn in his *Diary* tells us how he paid a visit to "old Lazarino Cominazzo," and got from him a carbine for which he paid a good deal of money. He seems to have been rather proud of his acquisition, as he more than once alludes to it.

The Civil War in England showed firearms in use with all four classes of lock. The infantry on both sides were chiefly armed with the heavy musket fired from a rest, having the match-lock. The cavalry had carbines fitted with snap-hances or the early complete flint, or were provided with wheel-locks.

The wheel-lock disappears from military arms about 1670, but continued in use in Germany for sporting rifles until a much later date. The *Flint-lock* proper came into use about 1630. The earliest specimens appear to be Spanish. The main-spring in these was on the outside of the lock-plate, and the mechanism of the simplest character, consisting of a catch forming a ledge, protruding to the outside of the lock-plate, for the foot of the hammer to rest on when cocked, and on this ledge being drawn back on pressing the trigger the hammer falls, striking the steel, which also covers the pan.

Fig. 41.—Richly Decorated Flint-lock. Probably Spanish. Collection of Major Farquharson.

Fig. 42.—Snap-hance of Italian make, about 1640. Collection of Major Farquharson.

The example Fig. 43 is one of a class where the ornamentation is very elaborate. The design is formed mostly by the chisel and hammer, and even in the internal mechanism the file appears scarcely to have been used. Many of these fine locks exist, but never have any armourer's mark on them; the mechanism, however, points to their Spanish origin. Works of this description were found in Spanish locks to the latter end of the eighteenth century. In both English and French flint-locks the mechanism was on the inside of the lock-plate, and a tumbler connected the hammer with the action of the mainspring. A later improvement was to add a bridle to give two bearings for the tumbler axle, and a small swivel connecting the tumbler with the mainspring, both of these improvements ensuring greater smoothness in the action. This form of improved mechanism was continued in the percussion lock, after the use of a flint was discontinued, and, indeed, the hammer used in the first military breechloader generally employed in our army, the Snider, was acted on by mechanism of much the same sort.

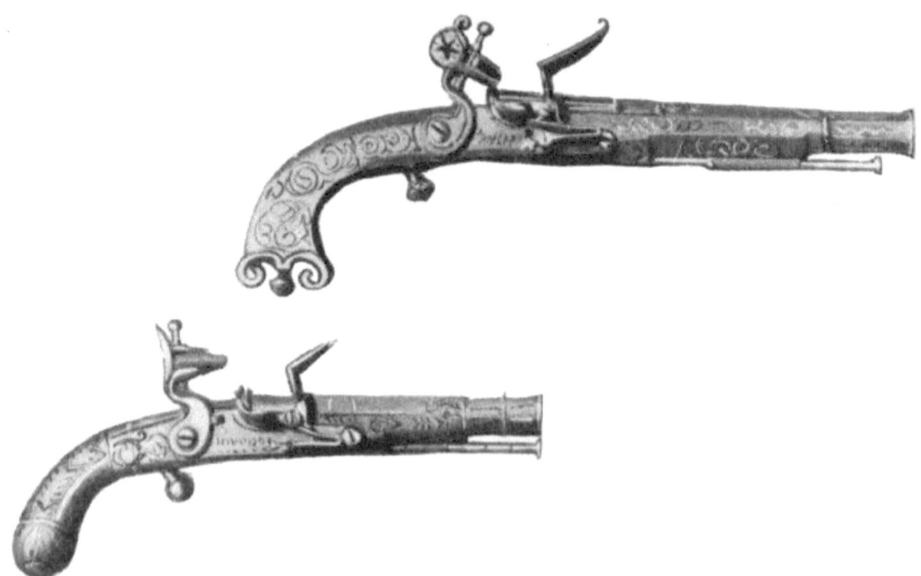

Figs. 43, 44.—Highland Pistols. Collection of Major Farquharson.

Figs. 43 and 44 show specimens of the Highland pistol, a class which stands quite by itself. These weapons no doubt were evolved from the early steel wheel dags in common use in Germany. Many Highlanders were to be found in the armies of other European nations, whence they probably took the fashion and also procured their firearms. The earliest weapons of the sort, as well as the latest, were all of steel (or rarely brass). The stocks had a heart-shaped butt, and were furnished with snap-hance locks. There is one of this description, undoubtedly a Scotch weapon, in the armoury in the old castle of Nürnberg, where the arms have always been stored, belonging probably to one of the many Scotch officers employed in Germany during the wars of the seventeenth century. Later on the butt of the pistol assumed a claw form and the ordinary flint-lock was employed, the mechanism, however, being of a distinctive sort, possibly of Dutch origin. The latest of these pistols have a rounded butt as in Fig. 44. The ornament found on the back of the hammer in Fig. 43 is not to be seen in any other class of lock.

The Highlanders looking at length on their weapons as part of the equipment of their national garb, a colony of armourers sprang up in the village of Doune in Stirlingshire, a place where "trysts" or fairs were held, and where the Highlanders resorted to exchange their cattle for other goods. The following account is given in *Scottish National Memorials*, of this trade of Doune. "The only remains of any of the ancient branches of trade is the making of Highland pistols. The reputation of Doune for this manufacture, about the time of the German war, was very great. This art was introduced to Doune about the year 1646 by Thomas Caddell, who having been instructed in his craft at Muthil, a village in Strathearn in Perthshire, came and settled at Doune. This famous tradesman possessed a most profound genius, and an inquisitive mind, and though a man of no education and remote from every means of instruction in the mechanical arts, his study and persevering exertions brought his art to so high a degree of perfection that no pistols made in Britain excelled or perhaps equalled those of his making either for sureness, strength, or beauty. He taught the trade to his children and several apprentices, of whom was one John Campbell, whose son and grandson carried on the business. While the ancient dress of Caledonia was worn, that is, the 'philabeg' belted-plaid, pistols, and dirk, the pistols made in Doune excelled all others, and acquired superior reputation over France and Germany; a pair superbly ornamented were fabricated by a tradesman taught in Doune, and by the city of Glasgow given in compliment to the Marquis de Bouillé. The above Mr. Campbell's grandson, who has now given over business, made pistols for the first nobility in Europe, as Prince Ferdinand of Brunswick, the Hereditary Prince of Brunswick, the Duke of Cumberland, and others. The trade is now (1798) carried on by John Murdoch (the maker of Fig. 44). These pistols were sold (1798) at from four to twenty-four guineas a pair."

The names of some of these armourers were the Caddells, James Sutherland, Thomas Murdoch, John Murdoch, S. Michie, John Campbell, J. Stuart, David M'Kenzie, and others. The trade died out at the commencement of this century.

These weapons were remarkable for grace of outline and great lightness. The butt has a small knob, which, when unscrewed, forms a picker to clear the touchhole with. The mainsprings in many cases appear to be weak, having little room to work in the slender stocks.

INDEX

Lector House believes that a society develops through a two-fold approach of continuous learning and adaptation, which is derived from the study of classic literary works spread across the historic timeline of literature records. Therefore, we aim at reviving, repairing and redeveloping all those inaccessible or damaged but historically as well as culturally important literature across subjects so that the future generations may have an opportunity to study and learn from past works to embark upon a journey of creating a better future.

This book is a result of an effort made by Lector House towards making a contribution to the preservation and repair of original ancient works which might hold historical significance to the approach of continuous learning across subjects.

HAPPY READING & LEARNING!

LECTOR HOUSE LLP
E-MAIL: lectorpublishing@gmail.com